IAN ALLAN TRANSPORT
LIBRARY

Birmingham Corporation Transport 1939-1969

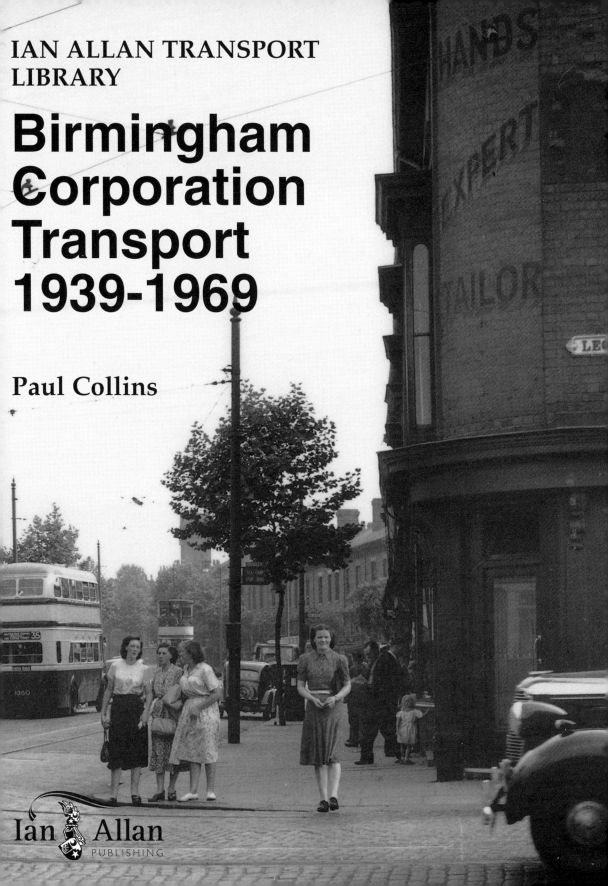

IAN ALLAN TRANSPORT
LIBRARY

Birmingham Corporation Transport 1939-1969

Paul Collins

Ian Allan
PUBLISHING

Contents

ACKNOWLEDGEMENTS

I am very grateful to the following individuals and organisations without whose help this book would not have been possible: the Staff at Birmingham Reference Library, June Collins, Ray Cresswell and Brierley Office Products, Louise Hampson, Mellanie Hartland, David Harvey, the library of the Ironbridge Gorge Museum Trust, Alan Mills and members of the Omnibus Society, and Rob Tarbass. I am also grateful to the following photographers for the loan of their work: G. H. F. Atkins, T. W. Moore, Ron Moss, R. H. G. Simpson, and R. J. S. Wiseman; and to the following photographers for being there at the right time: W. A. Camwell, D. W. K. Jones, V. C. Jones, R. Knibbs, Robert F. Mack, M. J. O'Connor, A. D. Packer, R. B. Parr, H. B. Priestley, D. A. Thompson, and Mike Waller.

I also wish to give special thanks to Nick Grant and Peter Waller at Ian Allan Publishing Ltd for their patience and forbearance, and to Winston Bond, Rosie Thacker, and Glyn Wilton of the National Tramway Museum for all of their help and support with this project.

Paul Collins MSc, MSocSc, PhD
Wollaston, Stourbridge, West Midlands

Front cover: The splendour that was Birmingham and its Corporation Transport. On Saturday 13 June 1964, Daimler CVG6 No 1875 of 1948/9 waits at traffic lights in Victoria Square before swinging round into New Street. The bus was withdrawn in 1968, and the buildings were demolished in 1969. They stood on the site of the former Christ Church, and are where the City's famous 'Floozy in the Jacuzzi' waterworks statue now reclines. *Ron Moss*

Back cover, top: Car No 670 of 1924 loads at Birmingham's last tram terminus in Steelhouse Lane, by the Gaumont Cinema, awaiting departure on route 79. *J. D. Mills*

Back cover, bottom: Daimler CRG6 Fleetline No 3393 was one of 48 (3351-3398) delivered from July 1964, and one of ten within this group to have an experimental windscreen. On 3 January 1965 the bus was working along Corporation Street, on the 39 service to Witton via Aston Cross. *T. W. Moore/IAL*

Half title: Resplendent with its Guy mascot, BCT wings, plus the odd dent or two, Guy Arab No 2609 waits for one of the crew to operate a Bundy time clock one day in February 1968. Stalwarts of the Outer Circle service, this Guy was not withdrawn until 1977. *T. W. Moore*

Title: Car No 408 swings out of Leopold Street into Moseley Road on 28 June 1949 to give chase to Leyland PD2 1660 working service 35 to the Maypole. This service, plus the tram and its route, last ran on 1 October 1949. *W. A. Camwell/National Tramway Museum*

Right: It wasn't just foreign visitors who were taken on trips around Birmingham by bus in 1966; one Corporation vehicle, Fleetline No 3575, went on tour to Lyon in France,

First published 1999

ISBN 0 7110 2656 4

Published by Ian Allan Publishing

an imprint of Ian Allan Publishing Ltd, Terminal House, Shepperton, Surrey TW17 8AS.
Printed by Ian Allan Printing Ltd, Riverdene Business Park, Hersham, Surrey KT12 4RG.

Code 9907/B

Introduction

This book, like its companion volume covering the years 1904-39, is an attempt to portray the working and development of Birmingham Corporation Transport — the largest municipally-owned transport undertaking in England. It has been compiled, in the main, from contemporary sources, and, in particular, from the Transport Department's own records. Unlike other histories of this kind, the focus is not primarily upon the vehicles, but upon the way in which this once mighty transport undertaking adapted itself to cope with changing times.

When this part of the story begins, Birmingham, like many other industrial towns and cities in Britain, was at war with an enemy who rained terror down from the skies. For much of the subsequent period covered by this volume, Birmingham was a city at war with itself, an almost perpetual building site, through which the Corporation's buses had to pick and thread their way. These upheavals are just some of the physical, social and political changes witnessed during this period, all of which are reflected here too.

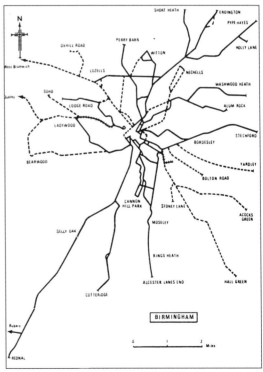

The Birmingham tram routes.

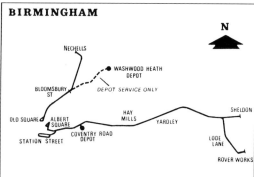

The Birmingham trolleybus routes.

Ultimately, this story is about people: the people of Birmingham who rode on the Corporation's trams, trolleybuses and buses, and the dedicated people of Birmingham who ran the same trams, trolleybuses and buses on their behalf. In 1948, Birmingham Corporation produced an illustrated booklet describing its transport undertaking under the heading *A Cavalcade of Progress*. Near its end, it was remarked that: 'Certainly the fact that Birmingham transport covers a distance equal to five times around the world *each day* must capture the imagination.' It is hoped, in telling the story of how this mighty task was achieved, that at least some of what follows might have a similar effect.

THE STORY SO FAR

The Birmingham Corporation Act, 1903, empowered it to operate its own tramways. A massive task of reconstructing and electrifying the tramways in a number of the city's districts lay ahead, as well as that of assuming operational responsibility for the other company-owned and worked tramway routes. The districts in question were: Aston; Balsall Heath; Perry Barr and Saltley; Dudley Road; Pebble Mill Road; King's Norton & Handsworth, and Small Heath. Of most pressing concern was the Aston route, which the Corporation was due to take over and operate from 1 January 1904.

On 1 October 1903 Birmingham Corporation made a significant appointment towards achieving all of this, when Alfred Baker, late Chief Officer of London County Council Tramways, was made General Manager of the newly formed Birmingham Corporation Tramways Department. Baker had seen the LCC through from the end of its horse tramways to the construction and inauguration of electrified routes using the conduit system, the first line of which had opened on 15 May 1903.

Practical arrangements delayed the opening of the tramways until 4 January 1904, when the Tramways Department commenced a service of tramcars between Steelhouse Lane and Aston Brook Street using 20 cars working from a new depot at Miller Street. Thereafter, new lines were added as the service grew to meet the transport needs of the city. Key dates in the development of Birmingham Corporation's transport service are:

- 1 January 1907 — Nine tramway routes were opened.
- 1 July 1911 — The Corporation gained complete control of the tramway services in its area as it assumed operation of the former City of Birmingham Tramway Co's routes.
- 1 January 1912 — The Corporation purchased and took over all of the former City of Birmingham Tramway Co's tramways.
- 19 July 1913 — Omnibus services were introduced as 10 vehicles were placed in service between Selly Oak and Rednal as an extension of the Bristol Road tramway.
- 15 October 1919 — Tramway track in Pebble Mill Road was relaid on a central reservation, the first of this kind of reserved track laid in the city. From this point until 1928 major extensions were made to the tramway system using this kind of construction.
- 27 November 1922 — Trolleybuses were substituted on the Nechells tram route; the first trolleybus-for-tram route conversion in the UK, and the first in the world to use double-deck top-covered vehicles.

Left: Further up Suffolk Street advertisement-free No 522 on Route 71 works its way back to Navigation Street. Out of the devastation in this part of the city wrought by the Inner Ring Road, just the building 'in front' of the tram survives.
L. L. Jones/Author's collection

Below: This line-up of eight Corporation buses inside Yardley Wood garage in 1943 is in a mixture of wartime grey and ordinary livery. the first three buses are Nos 396, 461 and 434, all AEC Regent 661s of 1930 or 1931. *L. W. Perkins*

- 1 March 1928 — Alfred Baker was replaced as General Manager by his son Arthur Chantrey Baker.
- 26 August 1928 — The tramway was extended from Bordesley Green East to Stechford along reserved track, the last major tramway extension of this kind built in the city.
- 4 May 1930 — Tramway services along Bolton Road Route 22 were replaced by omnibuses; the first omnibus-for-tram conversion in the city.
- 7 January 1934 — Yardley tramway services were replaced by trolleybus Routes 56, 57 (Hay Mills from High and Station streets), 92 and 93 (Yardley from High and Station streets). The services were operated by 49 new Leyland six-wheelers, with 58-seat Metropolitan-Cammell-Weymann bodies.
- 31 March 1936 — The financial year 1935-6 was an historic one for the Corporation transport undertaking. For the first time in its history the gross revenue from the omnibus service (£1,184,870) exceeded that from the tramways (£1,107,949).
- 31 March 1937 — End of year figures showed the omnibus service to be supreme in all statistics: miles run, passengers carried, number of vehicles and gross revenue.

At 11am on 3 September 1939, The Prime Minister, Neville Chamberlain, a former Lord Mayor of the City of Birmingham, declared war on Germany. As the citizens of Chamberlain's home city went about their lives that quiet late summer Sunday, they had one of the finest public transport systems ever to be developed in the United Kingdom at their disposal. It, like them, would be put to its greatest test in the six years of war that were to follow.

1. 1939-45: The War Years

Birmingham's industries, with their varied trades and a major role in motor vehicle and motor component manufacture, were destined to play a key part in the British war effort. Vital to this effort was the need to keep the city moving, and, in particular, to get workers to and from the factories. With the vast majority of people reliant upon public transport, Birmingham Corporation Transport played an indispensable role in this.

On the day war was declared, the Corporation could take pride in what it had achieved in developing its transport services. In the year ending 31 March 1939, Birmingham Corporation Transport vehicles had run almost 44 million miles in revenue-earning service, carrying 427 million passengers, bringing in almost £3 million in fares. It made a gross profit of just over £523,000 and employed nearly 9,000 people. All of this was set to change over the next six years of war, when the Corporation Transport service would face its greatest challenge.

On 10 January 1939 the City Council had approved a policy of the progressive abandonment of tramway routes as each became unremunerative, with trams being replaced by buses. An initial programme was approved that day, and

in the first month of the war one tram route was suspended, and two other groups of routes were withdrawn upon the expiry of leases. Thereafter, all further tramway abandonments were suspended for the duration of the war, as the realities of a conflict being fought on both overseas and home fronts sank in.

Although known piecemeal to those most intimately involved, the full extent of the wartime difficulties and losses suffered by Birmingham Corporation Transport were hidden from the public. The Transport Department's annual reports were shorn of their financial details, and of much information thought to have been useful to the enemy. When revealed after the war, it became clear that the darkest period had been the six months from November 1940 to April 1941; the time when the city endured the heaviest air raids, and the Transport Department suffered the most damage. One casualty was the Nechells trolleybus route, the country's first tram-to-trolleybus conversion, which fell foul of air-raid precautions because of the sparks it produced, and was withdrawn in 1940; but the following year the trolleybus system was extended, to serve a major new aero-engine plant.

With so many men away serving in HM Forces, vast numbers of women were employed to keep the transport service working. By the war's end nearly 7,500 women had been employed as conductresses, cleaners, drivers and works staff. Tramway services continued, and proved their reliability, but were vulnerable to air-raid damage to both their track and overhead. Buses proved their flexibility, but soon faced fuel rationing and service reductions, which led to increased fares. New buses were also in very short supply, and between 1942 and 1946 the Transport Department was allocated just 149 chassis by the Minister of War Transport, of which 84 were by Guy and 65 by Daimler, the latter comprising 55 CWA6s, 7 CWD6s, and 3 CWG5s.

By 1943 fuel had become so scarce that bus stops were 'thinned', and trials of producer gas as a substitute were imposed by the Ministry of War Transport. But there was also a glimmer of hope that the war might end, and that same year the city planners began to develop a scheme for building an Inner Ring Road around Birmingham, the eventual construction of which would change its character

Below left: The last prewar buses delivered to Birmingham Corporation were 50 Leyland TD6c 52-seaters (Nos 1270-319). No 1318, the penultimate in the batch, is seen at Victoria Square. It was withdrawn in 1952.
Roy Marshall/D. R. Harvey Collection

Below: Upon the declaration of war, one of the mainstays of Birmingham Corporation's bus fleet were the hundreds of Daimler COG5s delivered from 1934. One such was No 1057 of 1937 seen in the 1950s. It was withdrawn in 1960 and broken up in May 1963. *R. H. G. Simpson*

for ever. As an illuminated tram toured the city in May 1945 to celebrate Victory in Europe, Birmingham Corporation Transport had a proud record of war service, but any hopes that its immediate problems would be solved quickly were soon dashed.

1939: WIDER STILL AND WIDER

The first four months of the war gave a flavour of what was to come. Overall, the year also saw the withdrawal of six Morris Imperial double-deckers from 1933.

September — The bus garage at 65 Tennant Street (ex-BMMO) is closed, having been used by the Corporation since October 1914.

4 September — Upon the declaration of war, 1,170 men employed by the Transport Department, mostly reservists, are called up.

10 September — The Witton via Six Ways tramway Route 3 is suspended, not to be reinstated after the war. It is not replaced by a bus service.

30 September — The leases of the Smethwick and Dudley group of tramways expire and the services are withdrawn. This is the only wartime tramway closure in Birmingham. The routes affected are those operating from Rosebery Street depot: 29 (Bearwood), 30 (Windmill Lane, Smethwick), 31 (City-Soho via Heath Street), 55 (City-Grove Lane), 80 City-St Paul's Road, Smethwick), 85 (City-Spon Lane), 86 (City-Oldbury), 87 (City-Oldbury & Dudley), and from West Smethwick depot: 88 (Spon Lane-Windmill Lane). This change introduces joint working with the 'Midland Red', the Corporation working routes to Bearwood and Soho, outside the city boundary, in compensation. The withdrawn trams are replaced the

Top: The Smethwick and Dudley group of tram routes closed on 30 September 1939 with the expiry of the Corporation's lease on them. This was the only wartime tramway closure in Birmingham. Six months earlier, on 12 April 1939, car No 93 of 1906, passes the Grove Cinema in Dudley Road, Smethwick, as staff change the posters. The car was withdrawn from service later that month. *H. B. Priestley/National Tramway Museum*

Above: Birmingham Corporation's tram service to Dudley closed with the expiry of its lease on the route on 30 September 1939. Eleven months earlier, on 23 October 1938, an LRTL tour to Rednal began at Dudley, worked by top-of-the-fleet car No 843. *D. W. K. Jones/National Tramway Museum*

following day by bus services B82, B81, B83, B80, B85, B86, B87 and B88, the 'B' indicating joint working with the 'Midland Red.'

2 October — A series of fare adjustments is introduced.

9 November — The Transport Committee considers wartime lighting restrictions on road passenger vehicles. These are felt to be too severe, and a revised order is expected from the respective Ministries in January. Fuel is also rationed and cuts have to be made in bus service frequency, mainly by reducing services in the middle of the day, late in the evening and at weekends.

December — A system of War Wages comes into effect, increasing employment costs.

1940: INTO THE DARK

Air-raids, and the indiscriminate damage they caused, became an everyday occurrence in the first full year of the war. They also led to the withdrawal of an historic trolleybus service. In addition to these man-made hazards, at the end of January heavy snow falls put the Transport Department's snow clearing equipment to the test. They held 64 ploughs which could be fitted to trams, and 55 which could be fitted to buses, both of which were able to clear snow up to 3in deep, plus 19 salt and grit sprinklers which could be towed behind lorries. Deeper falls were tackled by nine large ploughs. The year saw no new buses delivered, and the withdrawal of one AEC Regent from

1930, one AEC Q double-decker from 1935, and the destruction by enemy action of six vehicles only delivered in 1939: five Leyland TD6c models and one Leyland TD7c.

19 January — The Lighting (Restrictions) Order, 1940, comes into force. This calls for the fitting of headlamp masks to buses and trams, and for the use of reduced lighting inside them. The latter is restricted to 0.1ft candles at seat level, and calls for the design of an intricate shade, which is produced by Mr P. W. Lawson of Kyotts Lake Road Repair Works. A total of 38,654 of these shades are made and fitted to the fleet, in addition to the 2,418 headlamp masks fitted to the buses and trolleybuses, and the 982 headlamp masks fitted to the trams.

March — Car 714, of the 702 class of 30 bogie cars acquired in 1925, overturns on the curve at the junction of Park Road and Witton Lane, injuring 30 passengers. The car is withdrawn from service and the fault traced to a cracked controller finger spring, combined with driver error.

31 March — The Transport Department's accounts for 1939/40 show that £18,260 has been spent converting Hockley tram depot for bus operation, and £103,321 on 50 buses as tram replacements. The other main vehicle purchase is 12 new Leyland TB7 trolleybuses, numbered 79-90 in the fleet, which cost £24,863.

19 May — A new bus service 10 is instituted between the City and Quinton Road West, Harborne.

2 July — In its annual report the Transport Committee records an expenditure of £35,000 occasioned by the 'heavy cost of Air Raid Precautions', and an extra £22,000 spent on fuel oil. It has also been instructed to devise a scheme which will provide free travel for members of HM Forces on leave in the city for more than 5 days.

15 August — A bomb falls at Anthony Road on Alum Rock Road, closing the Alum Rock tram route for three days.

17 August — A new scheme is introduced under which members of HM Forces in the city on leave for more than 5 days can ride on trams and buses free of charge. Tokens are issued, those of greater value being provided to service personnel living further from the city centre.

30 September — The Nechells trolleybuses service 7 is withdrawn due to wartime blackout problems caused by the pronounced flash the overhead equipment produces,

Above left: In 1940 Birmingham Corporation bought 12 new Leyland TB7 trolleybuses, Nos 79-90, at a total cost of £24,863. These were to operate an extension of the Sheldon service to an aero-engine factory in Lode Lane, Solihull, which began on 29 October 1941. Last of the fleet, No 90 is seen on this service on 17 June 1951, two weeks before it closed.
V. C. Jones/IAL

Left: As well as the war, the winter of 1939/40 brought heavy snow. Here snowplough-fitted 301 Class car No 307 of 1911 clears its path in Miller Street on 30 January 1940.
Author's collection

Above: 1940's snow persisted into February, and that month first in the fleet, car No 1 was on snowplough duties in Central Place whilst working Route 6. *Author's collection*

Left: The outward signs of war were headlamp masks and white fenders, as in this May 1940 picture of cars Nos 568, 559 and 581 seen in Miller Street Permanent Way Yard. *Author's collection*

Below left: Although fitted with some form of bow collector since 1924, on 8 June 1940 Brill car No 61 was photographed nosing its way into Rosebery Street depot, fitted with a trolley pole. Perhaps the 'Special' destination is a clue. These short-wheelbase cars were especially suited to the twisting Lodge Road route. *Author's collection*

Below: Twenty-two days later car No 61 was photographed back at work on the Lodge Road route, fitted with a conventional Rowland Skate bow collector. At left, the crew seem to be reading some instructions. *Author's collection*

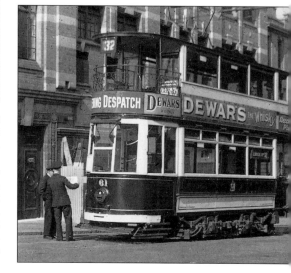

especially when returning to Washwood Heath depot using one trolley pole and a metal skate dragged along behind in the tram lines. The service is replaced by bus service 43, and is not reinstated after the war.

October — 30 AEC Regent 48-seat double-deck buses are loaned to London Transport until the end of November.

4 November — With an early blackout in force, work finishing times are altered to permit employees to travel home in daylight. This means that the Transport Department is carrying in one hour as many passengers as it usually carries in three. City centre loading places are

By 1941, large numbers of women had been taken on to cover for men on active service, mostly as conductresses. Their contribution to the war effort was recalled humorously by Harry Ward in this cartoon from the *Birmingham City Transport Gazette* of June 1946. *Author's collection*

split up to ease queuing, and as the shops become busier nearer Christmas, a loudspeaker van is employed to encourage shoppers to return home before 4.30pm.

19 November — An application is made to the Minister of War Transport to raise fares in order to cover a possible shortfall caused by the need to raise wages due to the war.

4 December — Five trams from the 301 class of 100 four-wheelers acquired in 1911 are destroyed in an air-raid on Witton depot. Also extensively damaged are nine cars from the 702 class of 30 bogie cars acquired in 1925, when part of the depot roof at the rear collapses on them. Officially held in reserve, none of these cars ever re-enters service, and they are eventually broken up in June 1945. Witton depot reopens in 1941, but it remains part roofless until 1947.

11 December — Henley Street Wharf is hit by a bomb.

1941: BLITZED

Unbeknownst to the public, The Transport Department suffered its worst year to date financially and in many other ways. A deficit in the year 1940/1 led to the first of many fare increases, a means that would eventually be resorted to each year. In early April, the city experienced one of the worst air-raids of the war, and its transport facilities took their share of this. One consequence was to accentuate the shortage of new vehicles, bringing about a formal suspension of the city's tramway abandonment programme. Large numbers of women were taken on to cover

for men on active service, and the trolleybus system was also extended, to serve an aero-engine factory. An immediate need for new buses led to the diversion of an order for four Daimler COG6s, with 8ft-wide 58-seat Metropolitan-Cammell bodies, originally intended for Johannesburg, to Birmingham Corporation. These were the first vehicles of this width to work in the city. Numbered 1320-3, they were not used in the city centre, but on the 18 service between Northfield and Yardley Wood. Only four new buses were acquired during the year: three Leyland Titan TD7 56-seaters (1324-6), and 1 Leyland Titan TD7 with a 56-seat Park Royal body (1327); and just one old vehicle disposed of, a Morris Imperial from 1933.

25 March — Sanction for the Transport Department's proposed fare increase is received from the Minister of War Transport. Fares up to 3d increase by ½d, whilst those over between 3½d and 5d are pegged at 4d; Workmen's returns rise 1d to 6d and children's fares are unaltered.

9/10 April — Birmingham suffers its worst air-raid of the war, and the tramway system receives 46 hits, some minor, some major. At Miller Street depot, 24 trams are destroyed: 18 are burned out, six so badly damaged that they are written off, and three more are withdrawn from service. Ten of the trams are from the first batch of 20 bogie cars purchased to open the Corporation's tramway service in January 1904, and they include car No 1; five are from the 512 class of 50 bogie cars acquired in 1913;

Above left: In 1941 the need for new buses was met in part by the diversion to Birmingham of a consignment of four Daimler COG6s (1320-1323) with 8ft-wide 58-seat bodies originally intended for Johannesburg. The first vehicles of this width to work in the city, they were not used in the centre but on the 18A service between Northfield and Yardley Wood, where No 1320 is seen at 'The Valley' on 13 September 1944.
L. W. Perkins/D. R. Harvey Collection

Above: The top deck of No 1283 was badly damaged when a bomb struck Harborne garage in 1940. It returned to service in 1941 with the top deck from withdrawn Morris Imperial No 553, but was withdrawn itself after sustaining the accidental damage shown, in 1949. *D. R. Harvey Collection*

Right: After the severe losses to the tram fleet suffered in April 1941 the Transport Department introduced a policy of night-time dispersal for some of the fleet. Here the Trinity Road football loop at Witton is being used to store 18 of the 301 class, headed by car No 353. *Author's collection*

eight from the 662 class of 40 bogie cars acquired in 1924, and one from the 702 class of 30 bogie cars acquired in 1925. Twenty more cars are also badly damaged in the same raid, including three more from the 1904 batch, leaving just six (Nos 3, 8, 13, 17, 18 and 20) in service. Four trams, from the second batch of 50 air-brake bogie cars (762-811) acquired in 1928, are also damaged in an air-raid on Washwood Heath depot.

1 July — In its annual report the Transport Department formally states that previously agreed tramway route abandonments have been suspended for the duration of the war. It also reports that there are currently 2,065 Department employees on active service with HM Forces, and that a large number of women have been engaged to cover for them. There are 2,104 conductresses, 351 cleaners and 69 engineers.

September — The Transport Department purchases 20 English Electric 54-seat double-deck bus bodies which are intended for an order of Daimler COG5 chassis placed by Manchester Corporation. The chassis had been destroyed in a bombing raid on the Daimler Works in Coventry. The bodies are used to recondition buses damaged beyond repair, and by June 1942 they enable 16 buses (12 Leyland TD6cs and four Daimler COG5s) to re-enter service. The four remaining bodies lead to the creation of a small pool of spare bodies which is used for major repair work up to November 1948.

Right: Buying English Electric 54-seat bus bodies, intended for an order of COG5 chassis placed by Manchester Corporation and destroyed in an air-raid on the Daimler Works, enabled 16 buses damaged beyond repair (12 Leyland TD6cs and four Daimler COG5s) to re-enter service. One recipient was Leyland Titan TD6c No 231, damaged in enemy action in April 1940, seen here, rebodied, at the terminus of service 69 in Lozells. *D. R. Harvey Collection*

Below: With the production of new buses strictly controlled during the war, the Transport Department had to rely upon its older vehicles to maintain the service. One such was Morris Imperial No 526 of 1933, seen after withdrawal in 1945 and disposal in May 1947. *R. H. G. Simpson*

29 October — The Sheldon trolleybus service is extended to Lode Lane, Solihull, as a special works service. It serves an aero-engine factory built by Rover as part of the second phase of the 'Shadow' Factory Scheme for the manufacture of Hercules radial aero-engines. The factory was constructed between June 1939 and September 1940, and the trolleybus service is subsidised by the Ministry of Works.

November — The Ministry of War Transport authorises the erection of 200 wartime bus shelters for use by passengers having to wait increased times owing to reduced services.

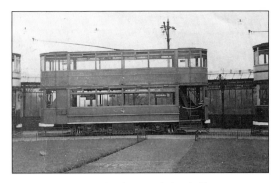

Above: Late in 1941 paint shortages led to the Transport Department using battleship grey, which was applied all over those buses and trams which needed painting, without any lining out. None of the air brake cars Nos 732-761 were thought to have been painted this way, but this shot of a car at Rednal in 1942 looks suspiciously like one of that class. *National Tramway Museum*

1942: VOLUNTEERS NEEDED

With around a quarter of the Transport Department's staff having been called up for HM Forces, the service had become increasingly reliant upon women workers and volunteers, with over 5,000 of both keeping the wheels turning. There was some good news too, with the delivery of 13 new vehicles: one Leyland Titan TD7 with a Northern Counties 56-seat body (1328); three 56-seater Leyland Titan TD7s (1329-31); six Guy Arabs with 56-seat Weymann bodies (1332-7); and three Daimler CWG5s with 56-seat Duple bodies (1338-40), the latter originally having no rear windows on the top deck. Only five older vehicles were withdrawn this year: one Morris Dictator from 1931 and four Morris Imperials from 1933.

May — The widening of part of Kings Road, Perry Barr, is completed. This has been undertaken so that a new bus service can be instituted to the Pheasey Estate, but the work has been delayed 23 months by Ministry of War Transport insistence that the cost of the works required be reduced from the original estimate of £9,998 to £6,540.

7 July — In its annual report, shorn of financial details owing to the war, the Transport Department records that 2,100 of its employees are currently on active service with HM Forces. In their place the Department is employing 2,576 conductresses, 376 women cleaners and 173 women as engineers. Other duties are being performed by part-time workers, which includes 359 conductors, 141 drivers, and 150 women cleaners. Volunteers are also engaged, with 2,150 auxiliary conductors working on voluntary service.

October — Car No 821, of the 30-strong batch of air-brake bogie cars (812-41) acquired in 1928, is withdrawn when it overturns after running away down the Pershore Road from Cotteridge terminus, becoming derailed at Breedon Cross. It had been parked without the handbrake being applied.

1943: LESS STOPS

Shortages extended from fuel to tyres, imposing reductions in both bus services and the number of stops they made. At Ministry insistence, trials also began with the use of producer gas as a fuel for buses. Looking ahead, the City planners made the first proposal for an Inner Ring Road. Meanwhile, vehicle deliveries increased, with 25 new buses: 18 Guy Arabs with 56-seat Weymann bodies and wooden slatted seats (1341-58), and seven Daimler CWA6s with 56-seat Duple bodies and wooden slatted seats (1359-65). Only two buses were withdrawn, both Morris Imperials from 1933.

21 February — Wartime economy measures are imposed on bus services to save fuel and tyre wear. In the evenings from 7.30pm services terminate outside the city's central loop, and other changes are made to the outer termini. These measures save the operation of 40,000 route miles each week. In addition, the number of bus stops per mile, previously six, is reduced to four.

June — Following a Ministry of War Transport instruction that 10% of all motorbus fleets over 100 strong must be equipped for operation with producer gas, the Transport Department has been conducting experiments with some of its vehicles on the Kingstanding route. Unfortunately,

At Cotteridge terminus a conductress swings the pole on top-of-the-fleet car No 843. The large cowl above the overhead covers a join in the overhead wire so that any electrical flashes which may occur at that point cannot be seen by enemy aircraft. *Author's collection*

the heavy city services which typify Birmingham are proving unsuitable for the gas-powered buses, which have to tow the producer gas equipment behind them on a trailer. The vehicles involved include 16 AEC Regent double-deckers acquired in 1931. None the less, it is noted that the basis of the trials is to equip the Department with the necessary skills and experience when and if fuel shortages become very serious.

6 July — The City Council's Public Works Committee submits a report on planning in the city centre. This has many recommendations concerning traffic and public transport:

• Traffic having no business in the centre has no business in the city, they conclude, and should be diverted 'by means of direct and convenient roads', recommending the construction of a 100ft-wide Inner Ring Road for this;
• Trams and buses should bring their passengers to within a reasonable distance of all parts of the city centre (300yd is suggested); and,
• Adequate bus loading places should be provided, with Colmore Row to be widened to 80ft and become the chief omnibus loading place for the city.

The Transport Committee's annual report, presented on the same day, notes that 2,028 of its employees are currently on active service with HM Forces. A total of 2,920 full-time women employees are working for the Department, with 2,380 as conductresses, 340 cleaners and 200 in engineering work. Use is still being made of part-time employees, with 397 conductors, 172 drivers and 259 cleaners, plus a further 1,500 auxiliary conductors working on voluntary service.

1944: TRAILER FAILURE; TOKEN SUCCESS
Birmingham's Transport Department could not be said to have been 100% behind the producer gas trials introduced in 1943; jokingly it could be said they weren't even 10% behind it! So its demise this year was not met with much sadness. A greater success was the Free Travel for HM Forces on Leave token scheme, which was reported on during the year. There was success too in the delivery of 46 new buses: 19 Guy Arabs with 56-seat bodies by Park Royal (1379) and Weymann (1366-78, 1380-4; Nos 1378 and 1384 had metal bodies with rounded corners to the windows); seven Daimler

Top left: Many of Birmingham Corporation's wartime buses were delivered with wooden slatted seats. This is the upper saloon of Guy Arab II 5LW No 1356, showing all but four of the 30 seats. *D. R. Harvey Collection*

Above left: The lower saloon of Guy Arab II 5LW No 1356, showing all but four of the 26 wooden slatted seats. *D. R. Harvey Collection*

Left: A number of the wartime buses delivered to Birmingham had short working lives with the Corporation. These included No 1345, a Guy Arab II 5LW of 1943, which was withdrawn from service in 1949 and was converted to a showman's towing vehicle. *R. H. G. Simpson*

CWA6s with 56-seat Park Royal bodies and upholstered seats and 20 Guy Arabs with 56-seat bodies by Park Royal (1393-1400, 1407-12), Strachans (1401-2) and Weymann (1403-6). These arrivals allowed 50 older buses to be disposed of: nine AEC Regents from 1929, 16 from 1930, 21 from 1931; Morris Imperials from 1933; plus one Daimler CP6 from 1933.

2 May — A petition has been received from residents in Belgrave Road, complaining about the speed of buses along there between Gooch Street and Moseley Road since the removal of a bus stop at Frank Street. The Transport Committee reports that the stop had been a request one, and rarely used, and was removed to comply with Ministry of War Transport instructions on reducing the number of stopping places. None the less, 'instructions have been given to drivers with regard to the speed of vehicles'.

end of May — Tokens to the value of £68,000 have been issued to members of HM Forces on leave in the city since the scheme was introduced on 17 August 1940.

4 July — In the Department's annual report it is noted that progress on the producer gas trials is still slow, and that Birmingham's experience with the trailers has been echoed by other operators. An industry-wide deputation has persuaded the Minister of War Transport to lower the stipulated percentage of vehicles required to be fitted for producer gas use from 10% to 5%. Commenting upon this, the Department notes, wryly, that whilst the city's reduced allocation of trailers will still have to be taken, there is no need to equip any more buses for producer gas operation as 'the life of a trailer does not appear likely to exceed nine months' service'. The number of Department employees on active service with HM Forces is 2,002 and there are 3,218 full-time women employees, com-

Above: In Navigation Street in May 1943 the Motorman and Conductress of car No 543 have spied the cameraman, whilst aboard car No 733 the blandishments for the Theatre Royal and Hippodrome seem more appealing. Even 'harmless' photography of this kind was heavily frowned upon during wartime. *Author's collection*

Below: During the war 6,000 vehicle windows were blown out during air-raids. At Alum Rock terminus on 20 July 1943, freshly painted air-brake bogie car No 775 has the scars of at least two of these breakages to view. *D. R. Harvey Collection*

Above: Blackout precautions are to the fore in this 1944 shot of the Bristol Road. Car No 587 is fitted with a headlamp mask, and both the tram buffers and traction poles have been painted white. *Birmingham Corporation*

Left: Ex-Birmingham Corporation No 1444 ended its days as a showman's towing vehicle. It had been one of 19 Guy Arab II 5LWs (Nos 1432-50), with 56-seat Park Royal bodies. On delivery they had slatted wooden seats, but these were progressively replaced with upholstered ones from withdrawn stock over 1946-8. The bus was withdrawn from service in 1949. *R. H. G. Simpson*

Above: In September 1944 the Minister of War Transport decreed that trials with producer gas trailers could cease. This view inside Yardley Wood garage on 15 September 1944 shows the discarded trailers behind AEC Regent No 368, ironically one of the few in its series not used for the producer gas trials. *L. W. Perkins/D. R. Harvey Collection*

Below: Some of the batches of 58 new Guy Arab II 5LWs delivered in 1944 were allocated to Yardley Wood garage, outside of which they are seen lined up on 1 November 1944. The lead vehicle is No 1403, one of four with Weymann bodies. *D. R. Harvey Collection*

Above: New Guy Arab II 5LWs peer into the autumnal sunlight from the entrance to Yardley Wood garage on 1 November 1944. Left to right are Nos 1437 and 1440, both with Park Royal bodies, then 1375, 1403 and 1376, with bodies by Weymann, and Park Royal-bodied 1439. *D. R. Harvey Collection*

Right: With white fenders, headlamp masks, and blast damaged windows, car No 722 works through the reserved track in Central Place in July 1944 on Route 3X. *A. W. V. Mace/National Tramway Museum*

prising 2,715 conductresses, 308 cleaners and 195 engineers. The part-time workforce comprises 282 conductors, 74 drivers and 280 cleaners.

26 July — Details of the city's Inner Ring Road Scheme are finalised at a marathon 5¾hr-long Council meeting. This will require the acquisition of 1,200 properties and 85 acres of land (at a cost of £12.1 million) and massive new road works (costing £2.5 million).

September — The Minister of War Transport decides that sufficient experience in the operation of producer gas-powered vehicles has been obtained and orders the experiments in its use to cease.

December — Car No 525 burns out while parked at Rednal terminus. The cause is traced to a cable fault.

1945: WAR RECORD

As the war drew to its end in Europe the City Council finalised its plans for the Inner Ring Road, which would change both the movement of traffic through the city, and the face of the city itself. The visible symbol of 'Victory' was an illuminated tram which toured the city, but later in the year the role played, and the price paid, by the Transport Department in the war was made public. There was also a

partial restoration of the services cut back during the war, and an early indication that the policy of tramway abandonment would soon be revived. A record 68 new buses were delivered: seven Daimler CWA6s with 56-seat Park Royal bodies (1413-19); six Daimler CWD6s with 56-seat Park Royal bodies (1420-5); six Daimler CWA6s with 56-seat Duple bodies (1426-31); 19 Guy Arabs with 56-seat Park Royal bodies and slatted wooden seats (1432-50); three Daimler CWA6s with 56-seat Duple bodies (1451-3); two Guy Arabs with 56-seat Park Royal bodies (1454-5); 24 Daimler CWA6s fitted with 56-seat bodies by Park Royal (1456-70, 1475-9) and Brush (1471-4); plus one Daimler CWD6 with a 56-seat Park Royal body (1480) — the last bus acquired by the Transport Department during the war. The arrival of these vehicles allowed 81 older vehicles to be withdrawn: one AEC Regent from 1929,11 from 1930 and 21 from 1931; 32 Morris Imperials from 1933; eight Daimler CP6s from 1933; one Guy Arab from 1934 and seven Daimler COG5s from 1935.

January — At the recommendation of the Town Clerk, the City Council seeks Parliamentary Powers to construct the Inner Ring Road.

30 April — Between this date and 27 August 1939, the Transport Department has provided 1,159 ambulance buses for the conveyance of 10,431 stretcher patients from hospital trains and the city hospitals to various other hospitals in the West Midlands. An additional 375 buses have been provided to carry 9,375 sitting patients. Most of this work has been undertaken by Department employees after completing their normal shifts, and, mostly, out of service hours.

May — A special 'Victory' illuminated tram is run around the city. It has been converted from car No 341 of 1911, which was reduced to a single-decker and adorned with 3,000 red, white and blue electric lamps, plus flags and a slogan, in March 1945. The slogan reads: 'VE Victory 1939 1945'. To reach those parts of the city cut off from trams, a similarly decorated illuminated bus is provided, based on No 1116, a Daimler COG5 of 1937.

25 June — With the ending of wartime restrictions, the time of last buses and trams from the city centre is moved from 10.30pm to 11pm.

July — The Ministry of War Transport announces that it is prepared to grant acquisition licences for buses built to prewar specifications. As a result of this ruling, the Transport Department places an order for 175 buses for delivery in 1946. During the war, the Transport Department has applied for 161 acquisition licences for wartime buses, and received 133 vehicles. With the war now over it has produced a revised body specification for these buses. They are to be fitted with upholstered seats, in place of the slatted wooden ones they have been delivered with, plus additional sliding windows. A new specification for postwar buses has also been produced that 'will incorporate a number of refinements which will add to the comfort of the passengers'.

3 July — With wartime restrictions lifted, the Transport Department makes public its accounts for the years 1940-1; 1941-2; 1942-3, and 1943-4. These show that in the depths of the war on the Home Front, during 1940-1,

the Department has actually had a net deficit on its accounts of £145,214 — a situation which was to be turned around by the next financial year. Over the same period the tram fleet has gone down by 25, and the bus fleet has increased by 87, with the trolleybus fleet remaining static at 90. Of the employees on active service with HM Forces, 111 have been killed, but 99 former prisoners of war have been liberated. Despite the end of the war in Europe, the transport service is still heavily reliant upon full-time women workers. Of the 3,588 women employed, 2,790 are conductresses and 798 work in skilled or semi-skilled occupations in the rolling stock department. Throughout the whole war, the Department has employed no less than 7,158 women.

Wartime damage has been considerable. The tramway track has been damaged in 70 locations by bombs, and the overhead has proven very vulnerable to blasts, often coming down in large sections as a result of explosions some distance away. In total, 41 trams and 20 buses have been completely destroyed by enemy action, 6,000 vehicle windows have been blown out and some 1,500 vehicles holed in explosions.

An early sign is also given that the full end to the war will bring a revival of the scheme to abandon the Lodge Road, Ladywood and Stechford tramways, permission to abandon these having been obtained on 10 January 1939. The Department also signals its intention to resume the erection of a motorbus garage at Quinton, and to convert the Rosebery Street tram depot to a bus garage in preparation for the Lodge Road and Ladywood tramway abandonments.

Below: Guy Arab II 5LW No 1401 was one of only two from its batch of 20 (Nos 1393-412) to be fitted with a body by Strachans. The batch was part of an order for 175 buses placed as the war ended to revitalise the fleet. *R. H. G. Simpson*

2. 1946-53: The End of the Electric Era

The service personnel resuming their work for Birmingham Corporation Transport after the end of the war returned to an undertaking beset by problems. As in so many other public services, the war had been won at some cost, and its legacy of worn-out vehicles and infrastructure would take some time to put right. There were many pressing problems, including:

• not all the staff on active service were returning to work, leaving a staff shortage;
• the bus fleet was inadequate to provide a prewar level of service;
• there was not sufficient garage accommodation to house all of the new buses required; and
• much of the tramway system had been used beyond its forecast replacement date and was badly worn.

Despite this pessimistic outlook, service innovations were implemented, and in April 1946 a long-awaited service of All-Night buses was introduced. Another bright moment came with the reintroduction of the staff magazine, suspended for the war, but when a survey of the bus fleet showed over 30% of it to be more than 10 years old, some measure of the task ahead was gained.

January 1947 saw the introduction of the five-day week, the first of a series of legislative changes that would significantly raise employment costs for the Transport Department. That year also saw the revival of the tramway abandonment policy, with the closure of two groups of routes, but the replacement buses were delivered too slowly, so an interim arrangement of reconditioning 110 prewar vehicles was reached. Another group of tram routes closed in 1948, the year also seeing a fully planned proposal for an underground railway system for the city, which was defeated by its costs.

By 1949, the Corporation's Transport Committee had ordered 1,100 buses, but only 320 of them had been delivered. As most of these were needed to replace trams, their slow delivery rate was a major factor in planning a pro-

gramme for the final abandonment of tramway operation in the city. For those who loved Birmingham's trams, Tuesday 5 July 1949 was a fateful day, for it was then that the final tramway abandonment programme was announced. Birmingham's last tram would run on 1 July 1953. Sadly too, the city would not run its last tram under the General Manager whose father had inaugurated the service in 1904; Mr A. C. Baker died in July 1950. The tramway abandonment policy included the remaining trolleybus services, which closed in June 1951, and the first Saturday in the Julys of 1952 and 1953 saw the last trams

Left: A service of All-Night buses was introduced on 15 April 1946, and this striking artwork graced the cover of the fold-out time-table and route map issued to accompany the launch. *BCT/Author's collection*

Above and right: Upper and lower saloon views of No 1235, a Daimler COG5 of 1939, rebuilt with a 54-seat body by Brush as a prototype for postwar vehicles. The all-metal body had a less rigid mounting system, incorporating rubber to absorb vibration, and a lowered centre of gravity, in the hope of a 12-15 year trouble-free life. This was 1946's only bus delivery. *Brush Coachwork Ltd/IAL*

run on the Bristol and Pershore roads, and then on the routes through Aston to the northeast of the city, with the last trams of all.

Between 1947 and 1953 Birmingham took delivery of 412 Daimler CVG6 buses, 162 of which had bodies by Metropolitan-Cammell, and 250 with ones by Crossley. It also received 513 additional Daimlers, 438 CVD6s with Daimler engines, and 75 CVA6s with AEC engines, all with Metropolitan-Cammell bodies. The last 250 CVG6s and 150 CVD6s each received the Corporation's new front styling, with the radiator totally enclosed behind a grille.

There were also a small number of AEC Regent III chassis, with Park Royal bodies.

1946: ALL NIGHT LONG

Three decisions by the Minister of War Transport boosted the Transport Department, as restrictions on bus ordering were lifted; these could be 8ft in width if desired, and sanction was also given for the abandonment of the Lodge Road and Ladywood tram routes. A new service of All-Night buses was introduced, and shelved plans for a bus garage at Quinton were dusted off. The Parliamentary Act authorising construction of the Inner Ring Road also became law. There was just one bus delivery in the year, a Daimler COG5 of 1939 (No 1235), rebuilt with a 54-seat body by Brush as a prototype for postwar vehicles. The all-metal body was designed with several innovative features, including a less rigid mounting system incorporating rubber to absorb vibration, and a lowered centre of gravity. It was hoped that the body would give a trouble-free life of 12-15 years. The bus entered service in the spring. In all, 22 buses were withdrawn from service: one AEC Regent from 1931; two Morris Imperials from 1933; three Daimler COG5s from 1934 and 16 Daimler COG5s from 1935.

January — Trams Nos 49 and 254, two of the 17 survivors from the 130 four-wheel cars acquired in three batches between 1905 and 1908, are withdrawn, sold and broken up.

1 January — Wartime restrictions on the ordering of new buses are lifted.

11 February — The Minister of War Transport announces that public passenger vehicles of 8ft in width can operate on suitable roads. In response, Birmingham Corporation changes the specification of the 175 vehicles it ordered towards the end of 1945 so that they can be of this width.

26 February — The Chief Engineer of the Transport Department, Mr T. C. E. Rowland, retires after 40 years' service. He has been Chief Engineer since March 1928 and is replaced by the Chief Assistant Engineer, Mr H. Parker.

9 April — The Transport Committee reports that the return of employees from active service with HM Forces has seen 1,250 men resume their duties with the Department. This has enabled 800 conductresses to be replaced, and for no more to be engaged, and for all voluntary and auxiliary staff to be dispensed with.

Approval has also been received from the Minister of War Transport for the conversion of the Lodge Road and Ladywood tram routes to bus operation.

Garage accommodation for buses is proving inadequate. The Transport Committee reports that this problem is so acute that 52 vehicles are being parked in the streets each night. As a matter of urgency the resumption of con-

struction of a new garage at Quinton is sought. A site for this, at the junction of Ridgacre Road and Ridgacre Lane, had been acquired just on the outbreak of war, but the scheme had been shelved. The garage would accommodate 100 buses and cost an estimated £119,000, of which £76,500 would be for the brickwork, £23,000 for the steelwork, £14,000 being for machinery and plant, the balance being fees. Sanction is given to borrow the necessary money to complete the scheme.

15 April — After an extensive census, the Transport Department allows the experimental introduction of All-Night buses on 16 routes, plus one between Great Barr (Scott Arms) and New Street via Summer Lane, to be operated by the 'Midland Red'. Although the census had shown that 'there was no great amount of night traffic in the city', it is felt that the provision of such a service will get around the need to provide special facilities for Service personnel, social functions, railway excursions, and will assist in the transportation of the Department's employees to and from duty. All of the buses will operate to and from

BIRMINGHAM CITY TRANSPORT GAZETTE

MAY, 1946

VOL. I . No. I

Left: The striking cover for the revived series of the *Birmingham City Transport Gazette*, relaunched in May 1946. It had a reasonable shelf-life too; tram Route 2 was one of the last to close in July 1953. *Author's collection*

Above: Harry Ward's cartoon for the first issue of the relaunched *Birmingham City Transport Gazette* introduces some of the Department's personalities, including the General Manager, A. C. Baker. *Author's collection*

the city centre, and will be timed to leave at 11.30pm, midnight, 1am, 2am, 3am, 4am and 5am, with additional 6am and 7am services on Sundays. The service will be tried initially for six months and then reviewed.

30 April — No further need is seen to continue providing free travel to members of HM Forces on leave in the city, and it is withdrawn from this date. Up to 31 March 1946, tokens to the value of £133,000 have been issued. Service personnel still in receipt of medical care and travelling in 'Hospital Blue', will continue to be able to travel free.

17 May — Publication of the monthly *Birmingham City Transport Gazette, The Official Organ of the Birmingham City Transport, Social, Athletic and Thrift Society* resumes under the Honorary Editorship of Richard Taylor. This has been suspended since 1939, and reappears in a new series from Vol 1 No 1. The *Gazette* had its origins in a magazine issued for 2½ years before World War 1, but which was revived in 1926 under the editorship of F. G. Hopton. Both these and the revived issues are enlivened by skilful and witty cartoons by Harry Ward. Issue 1 is full of Branch reports about reunions with staff returning from active service. Selly Oak are particularly pleased to welcome back a colleague known affectionately as 'Soggy' Rainbow!

2 July — The Transport Committee's annual report shows that the Department currently has 462 trams, 1,202 buses and 74 trolleybuses in its fleet, and that the major item of expenditure for the year was £78,942 1s 11d on new buses. A further £20,628 has been spent in transferring the sand drying plant from Sampson Road Wharf, where the lease had expired, to a new site in New Bond Street. Offset against this was £5,000 received from the sale of the old buildings at Sampson Road.

The age of the bus fleet is giving most concern to the Committee. An audit has shown there to be 316 vehicles in service over 10 years old, and 684 over 8½ years old. A programme involving the replacement of 275 buses a year for 3 years from 1947 is deemed necessary 'if the fleet is to be maintained efficiently'. Tenders have been advertised for this programme, which is estimated to cost £1,064,000 per annum.

A review of the All-Night bus service shows that it is fulfilling a public need, and the experiment is therefore extended from six to 12 months, when it will be reviewed again.

Consideration has also been given to offering free travel to Old Age Pensioners. Forty other transport operators have been canvassed for accepted practice on this. Of these 33 offer no concessions whatsoever, and 7 grant limited ones during 'slack hours' to pensioners over 70, mainly on journeys to the nearest Post Office to collect their pension. It is also understood that the Government is likely to increase pension rates shortly, and so it is decided that it would 'be inappropriate to make any concessions'.

Sufficient time has now elapsed for the meritorious war service of the Department's employees to be reported in full, and the following figures are given:

• No of employees on war service	2,129
• No returning to the Department	1,439
• No killed on active service	138
• No disabled and discharged	36
• No now employed elsewhere	312
• No still to return	186

1 August — The Bill authorising the city to construct the Inner Ring Road gains the Royal Assent, but it will be another 11 years before construction work actually begins.

1947: LIGHTER TRAMS

With the New Year came the five-day week, which raised the Transport Department's employment costs by almost £250,000 a year, although savings were expected following the closure of the Lodge Road tram routes in March and the Ladywood route in August. At its annual review, the All-Night bus service was looked upon favourably and allowed to continue, and plans were prepared for another new bus garage, this time at Lea Hall. New bus deliveries started to come through in quantity, the year seeing a prototype Leyland PD2, with a 56-seat body (296); 75 Daimler CVA6s with AEC engines, and 54-seat Metropolitan-Cammell bodies (1481-1555); 75 Daimler CVG6s, with Gardner 6LW engines and 54-seat

Below left: A triptych of cartoons illustrating a report in the *Birmingham City Transport Gazette* on the last Lodge Road trams on 30 March 1947. The one on the right records the souvenir hunting which took place on the last car. *Author's collection*

Above: New Daimler CVA6 No 1501 looks resplendent as it works the 10 service out of the city to Quinton Road West in September 1947. It was one of 75 such Daimlers, with AEC engines and 54-seat Metropolitan-Cammell bodies (Nos 1481-555). *G. H. F. Atkins*

Right: From the second batch of Daimler CVG6s delivered in 1947 (Nos 1556-630), No 1577 is seen in the rain at Cotteridge, on a special working on 7 August 1949. The bus was withdrawn in 1962. *V. C. Jones/IAL*

Above: The Technical College in Navigation Street towers above Daimler CVG6 No 1598 of 1947. Excellent overviews of the surrounding streets could be taken from the college's windows, but it was demolished with the rebuilding of New Street station. The bus was one of 75 with Gardner 6LW engines and 54-seat Metropolitan-Cammell bodies (Nos 1556-630). *R. H. G. Simpson*

Right: Between May and August 1947, Rosebery Street depot was converted into a bus garage. Initially, it received most of the Leyland TD7cs in the Nos 1270-319 batch, two of which, Nos 1292 and 1312, can be seen here, along with cars Nos 345 and 736. *D. R. Harvey Collection*

Metropolitan-Cammell bodies, (1556-1630); 15 AEC Regent IIIs with 54-seat Park Royal bodies (1631-45); and the start of a body refurbishment scheme for 110 prewar vehicles. Withdrawn from service were eight AEC Regents from 1931; one Morris Imperial from 1933; 19 Daimler COG5s from 1934 and 60 Daimler COG5s from 1935.

6 January — The introduction of a 44hr, 5-day working week in the Engineering Industry has immediate repercussions for the Transport Department in two ways. As a large employer, employment costs are predicted to rise by £242,000 in 1947, and as the carrier of other people's employees, there is a marked falling off in passenger journeys on Saturday mornings. It is hoped that the latter may even out in the summer months, when those not working on Saturdays will make 'pleasure journeys'.

30 March — The last Lodge Road Route 32 car runs into Rosebery Street depot just after midnight, driven by Motorman David Harwood, with Conductor Walter

Above: Under the direction of a point-duty policeman, Daimler CVG6 No 1604 turns whilst working the 28 service to Great Barr in the early 1960s. It was one of 75 buses (Nos 1556-630) delivered in 1947, that gave nearly 20 years' service. The last was withdrawn in 1966; No 1604 went in 1963.
R. H. G. Simpson

Billingham. A large crowd has gathered at Lodge Road terminus and at other points on the route. Souvenir hunters are busy on the car with screwdrivers and penknives, and, as the *Transport Gazette* describes, 'it was a very incomplete vehicle when it arrived at its last destination'. Conversion of the Ladywood route, sanctioned at the same time, has been delayed pending the final adaptation of Rosebery Street depot for buses and the delivery of the necessary vehicles. Buses on a new service 96 replace the Lodge Road trams the following day. As a result of this closure, the remaining 15 cars, from the 130 four-wheelers acquired between 1905 and 1908, are withdrawn. The body of one, No 266, becomes PW8, and the last tram to operate in Birmingham.

1 April — The Transport Committee reports it is now opportune to substitute buses for trams on the Stechford route. An additional 35 vehicles will be needed for this, which will be added to the order for 1948, itself already

increased to 300 from the planned 275 to allow for the withdrawal of most of the 302 buses which have been in service for 10 years or more. These 335 buses are estimated to cost £1,256,000.

Reviewing the All-Night bus service after its first year, the Transport Committee decides that it should continue as an experiment for an additional 12 months. Every effort will also be made to restore a full ordinary service up to the start of the All-Night buses at 11.30pm.

Formal sanction is finally given to the withdrawal of the Nechells trolleybus service, officially 'suspended' since 30 September 1940. The replacement bus service will continue in its stead, but it is also noted that: 'the old trolley vehicles have been scrapped by reason of their age, and part of the overhead equipment has been utilised in other parts of the city', which would have made reinstatement of the service very difficult.

1 July — The Transport Committee reports that plans are being prepared for the erection of a bus garage in Lea Hall. Before the war a site for this had been acquired at the junction of Crossfield Road and Kitts Green Road. The garage will accommodate 100 vehicles and is estimated to cost £175,000.

15 July — The Transport Committee consider tenders for the 335 buses reported to Council on 1 April. Allowing

Above One of the last of the 1947 Daimler CVG6s to be withdrawn in 1966 was No 1596, seen here in Navigation Street in the early 1960s. The tarmac the bus is standing on the patched road after the removal of the tram lines 10 years earlier. *R. H. G Simpson*

Below: Freshly delivered AEC Regent III No 1634 was one of 15 fitted with 54-seat Park Royal bodies (Nos 1631-45). In September 1947 it was working the 1 service City-Moseley Village. *G. H. F. Atkins*

Above: The 15 Park Royal-bodied AEC Regent IIIs (No 1631-45) delivered in 1947 worked on into the 1960s. Shortly before withdrawal in 1963, No 1644 is seen passing a UCP restaurant, a chain which specialised in tripe dishes, popular in the war as meat coupons were not needed for them. *R. H. G. Simpson*

Left: Leyland only ever built two PD2s, and Birmingham had the second of them. Numbered in series with Leylands Nos 211-95 of 1938, No 296 entered service on 29 September 1947. It gave reliable service for 30 years and was photographed, having passed under the Ryland Aqueduct at Dudley Port, on 18 October 1964, remaining in service until 31 October 1967. *G. Kellard/IAL*

for price increases between the time of order and delivery, it is estimated that an additional £146,787 will have to be added to the overall cost of the contract.

30 August — The Ladywood tram Route 33 closes; it is replaced by bus service 95 the following day, when Rosebery Street depot becomes a bus garage. This closure also results in the withdrawal of five trams from the 301 class of 100 four-wheelers acquired in 1911.

December — Owing to the slow delivery of new buses, and the urgent need to convert tram routes to bus opera-

tion, the Transport Department enters into a contract with Samlesbury Engineering Ltd for the reconditioning of 110 prewar vehicle bodies, all of which were built by Metropolitan-Cammell. This month buses 972 and 991 are sent to Samlesbury's and return as chassis, followed by two more in January 1948, and 10 more that February. The reconditioning scheme will take until July 1949 to complete. Most of the vehicles will retain their original bodies, but 15 will return with a different body from the one they went with.

Above: Leyland PD2/2 No 1732 was one of 100 such buses (1656-755) with 54-seat Brush bodies delivered in 1948. It is seen here loading outside the Town Hall in Colmore Row on 13 June 1964. *Ron Moss*

Left: Nationalisation was in the air in 1948. The Corporation's Electricity Department had been taken over, and Harry Ward caught the mood well in this cartoon for the *Birmingham City Transport Gazette*. The caption read 'You ought to have got off at the last stop, Madam.' 'I ought'er got off at the last stop, eh! The Government ought'er take you over, then p'raps I could tell you where to get "off".' *Author's collection*

Above right: The 100 Leyland PD2/1s (Nos 1656-755) delivered in 1948 gained a great reputation for reliability, and 1709 looked remarkably smart too as it waited in Victoria Square on 13 June 1964. There were four more years of service for the bus, which was withdrawn in 1968. *Ron Moss*

Right: Coventry Road depot, with car No 326 departing on route 84 and car No 314 approaching, whilst in the distance a trolleybus, possibly No 50, works on out to Sheldon. The closure of the Coventry Road tram routes on 2 October 1948 allowed the withdrawal of 38 of the 301 Class trams, including the two seen here. *Author's collection*

1948: UNDERGROUND, OVERGROUND...

A programme to remove one of the more visible legacies of the war, the bombed-out buildings in the city, was completed this year, and in an attempt to speed up traffic in the centre, horse-drawn vehicles were banned during the morning and evening peaks. Redevelopment plans for the city included an underground electric railway, and the Council lost control of one of its most important assets, the Electricity Department, when that industry was nationalised. New buses were still slow being delivered, but sufficient were received to permit the closure of the Coventry Road tram routes. The new vehicles were: 10 Crossley HOE7s with 54-seat bodies (1646-55); 100 Leyland PD2s with 54-seat Brush bodies (1656-55) and 88 Daimler CVD6s with 54-seat Metropolitan-Cammell bodies (1756-843). These allowed 133 older buses to be withdrawn: 37 Daimler COG5s from 1934; 50 Daimler COG5s from 1935; 38 Daimler COG5s from 1936; 3 Daimler COG5s from 1937 and five Leyland TD4cs from 1937.

March — The first stages in the emergence of a new city are completed by the removal of 6,985 war-damaged buildings and the making safe of 600 others. To date this work has cost £60,000, but has been delayed by Ministry of Health insistence that the owners of the buildings give their consent to the demolition or works. Sadly, many of the owners cannot be traced. A report by the Traffic Advisory Committee also notes that horse-drawn traffic reduces speeds in the city centre from 9mph to 2mph. In the light of this, British Railways agree not to use horse drawn vehicles on the one-way City Ring between 8.30am

and 9.30am, and 5.30pm and 6.30pm, and, subsequently, the Council abandons the use of such vehicles in the city centre, except in an emergency.

31 March — The Transport Committee's annual accounts show that the fleet currently comprises 440 trams, 1,262 buses and 74 trolleybuses. It also notes that the 'future financial position of the Undertaking gives cause for anxiety in view of the constantly increasing cost of operation'. Amongst the concerns voiced are ones over the increasing cost of employment, with changes in working hours and statutory wage increases, and the introduction of loan charges. The total expenditure on war damage is now £128,666, for which no contribution has so far been received from the War Damage Commission.

1 April — The City of Birmingham Electric Supply Department is formally transferred to the ownership and control of the Midlands Electricity Board. Certain of the Electricity Department's assets stand on land controlled by the Transport Department, such as the substations at the

Below: As the tramway abandonment programme continued there was a growing need to train former tram crews and new employees to drive buses. At the junction of Cattell and Coventry roads, Guy Arab II 5LW No 1408 is on a special learner duty. *D. R. Harvey Collection*

Right: Postwar recovery is bringing more and more vehicles on to the roads, particularly in the city centre, in this view of Corporation Street in 1948. Trams from Martineau Street also used this road for two more years. *D. R. Harvey Collection*

Tramways Stadium in Kings Heath, and at Hockley Garage. These are not formally transferred to the Board until the middle of 1950.

3 May — A new bus service, the 28A, is introduced between Station Street, Small Heath and Great Barr (Dyas Road).

6 July — The Transport Committee's annual report notes that difficulties in obtaining buses has meant that tramway services have had to be continued longer than anticipated. Of the 785 buses ordered to date, only 210 have been delivered, and there are now 550 vehicles which have been in service for 10 years or more. Maintenance costs on the remaining trams and track are also high, and the severe winter of 1947 has added considerably to the Permanent Way bill, which is £89,777 for 1946/7. Wage awards and reductions in working hours are producing additional concerns over the financial viability of the transport service, and the likelihood of a fares increase is mooted. Subject to being able to obtain sufficient replacement buses, the Transport Committee signals its intention to convert the Moseley group of tramways, Routes 37, 39, 40, 41, 42 and 48, to bus operation. Sixty vehicles will be required to make this possible, which, combined with 250 needed to replace older buses and 50 needed for increased traffic, brings the requirement to 360, which will cost £1,620,000.

The City Surveyor has also investigated the feasibility of constructing an underground electric 'tube' railway to serve northeast Birmingham (Perry Barr, Kingstanding, Erdington, Aston). An extensive study has been made of London tube railways, and a scheme to construct 11 miles of such a line has been developed. Stations are envisaged at Aston Cross, Salford Bridge, Erdington High Street, Perry Common, Kingstanding, Perry Barr and Hockley. A 5min interval peak and 10min interval off-peak service is proposed, with an average fare of 4d. It is estimated that 57,000 passengers would use such a line each day, but the proposals come unstuck when the economic aspects are studied. With an overall capital cost of £13.75 million, annual income is calculated at just £350,000, which, allowing for loan charges and operating costs, produces an estimated annual deficit of £831,800 per annum, so the scheme is abandoned.

29 August — The 15B bus service is extended along Garretts Green Lane to Sheldon Heath Road.

October — Birmingham Corporation publishes an eight-page commemorative two-colour booklet: *BIRMINGHAM CITY TRANSPORT A Cavalcade of Progress*, containing an article entitled 'FORWARD The Story of the Largest Municipally-Owned Transport Undertaking in England'. Taking as its start the year 1828, when 'the cobbled streets of Birmingham echoed to the ring of horses' hooves and the metalled wheels of the city's first omnibus', it tells the story of how public transport in the city developed into 'a municipal transport system second to none in scope and efficiency'.

2 October — Closure of the Coventry Road tram Routes 11 (City-Bordesley Green via Fazeley Street), 12 (City-Bordesley Green via Deritend), 84 (City-Stechford via Deritend) and 90 (City-Stechford via Fazeley Street). They are replaced by bus services 51, 52, 54 and 53 the following day. The city terminus of the replacement bus services is switched from Albert Street to Carrs Lane. This closure allows 20 trams from the 301 class of 100 four-wheelers acquired in 1911 to be withdrawn. They are broken up at Moseley Road depot by January 1949.

14 October — Following a petition from pensioners in Aston the subject of free travel is broached again. Once more the Transport Committee can see no need to offer this concession.

1949: A NEW FACE

Early in the New Year the Transport Department received sanction for a fares increase, which it hoped would ease its financial situation, made ever worse by increased employment costs. With buses now being delivered more quickly, a programme of tramway and trolleybus abandonment could also be planned, and was announced this year. As a consequence of this, the Moseley group of tram routes was closed and some older trams withdrawn. A regular bus service began to Elmdon Airport from a newly established air terminal in the city, and Transport Department designers and bus makers worked together to produce a new front end design for the city's buses. Excellent progress was also made on the new Quinton bus garage, which opened towards the end of the year. The new vehicles delivered

included 87 Daimler CVG6LWs with 54-seat Metropolitan-Cammell bodies (1844-930) and 100 Daimler CVD6s with 54-seat Metropolitan-Cammell bodies (1931-2030). In total, 196 older buses were withdrawn: 11 Daimler COG5s from 1934; 33 Daimler COG5s from 1935; 24 Daimler COG5s from 1936; 63 Daimler COG5s from 1937; four AEC Regents from 1937; 36 Daimler COG5s from 1938; nine Leyland TD6cs from 1939; 14 Daimler COG5s from 1939 and two Leyland TD7cs from 1939.

4 January — The Transport Committee reports that, as predicted last July, an increase in fares is necessary. Permission has been obtained from the Minister of Transport to raise fares between 1d and 3½d by ½d, but to reduce those above 4d to that level; workmen's fares are to rise from 5d to 6d. These changes will be introduced later in the year. Orders have now been placed for 1,145 buses, of which only 320 have been delivered. The limitation is a Government restriction on the building of new buses, which limits production to 3,650 vehicles in 1948 and to 4,250 in 1949. Given that these are national figures, the Committee feels it is receiving a reasonable quota of new vehicles. With ministerial sanction having finally been obtained, good progress is now being made on the erection of a bus garage in Ridgacre Road, Quinton.

20 March — The 15A bus service is extended along Queens Road and Wheatcroft Road to Whittington Oval.

Above: The 10 Crossley double-deckers (1646-55) delivered in 1949 were the first buses supplied to the Corporation by that manufacturer. The first of the batch of 54-seaters is seen on service 55 in the early 1960s; they were all withdrawn in 1964. *R. H. G. Simpson*

Above right: Steelhouse Lane was destined to become the city's last tram terminus, but in 1949 that was three years off. Car No 642 of 1923 waits by the old Wesleyan & General Assurance Office to work Route 2, while Daimler COG5 No 1239 of 1939 runs past. *J. Whybrow/Robin D. Tarbass Collection*

31 March — The Transport Committee's annual report shows that the fleet currently comprises 412 trams, 1,288 buses and 74 trolleybuses. The accounts for 1948/9 show a gross profit of £316,515. There has been considerable expenditure from loans during the year, the main item being £919,359 on buses.

April-July — Transport Department designers begin work with bus manufacturers to create a front design for the Corporation's new generation of tram-replacement buses. Much of this work is undertaken by Guy, and the design features a radiator concealed behind a grille.

8 May — The 13A bus service is extended along School Road from Priory Road to its junction with Ravenshill Road.

29 May — The 14 bus service is extended from Lea Village, along Kitts Green Road and St Giles Road to Haywood Road to serve the Tile Cross Estate, and two short workings of the service are introduced: the 14A to Glebe Farm Road, and the 14B to Lea Village.

5 July — On 7 July 1936 the City Council resolved that tramway routes which proved to be unremunerative would be abandoned. The Transport Committee reports that it now considers all of the city's remaining tram and trolleybus services to fall into that category, and that a programme of tramway and trolleybus abandonment has been drawn up:

- 1 October 1949   Moseley group of routes 37, 39, 40, 41, 42 and 48
- 1 January 1950   Perry Barr (6) and Witton (3X) routes
- 1 October 1950   Lozells (5), Alum Rock (8) and Washwood Heath (10) routes
- 1 July 1951   Coventry Road trolleybus services 93 and 94
- 1 July 1952   Pershore Road (36) and Bristol Road group 70 and 71
- 1 July 1953   Erdington group of routes 2, 78, 79

To achieve this programme 425 additional buses will be required. Of the trolleybuses, the Committee makes reference to the fact that their introduction had been 'to gain experience of the operation of these vehicles' and that 'the results have not been such as to influence your Committee in extending the use of this type of vehicle'. The Ministry of Transport, which until recently had been advocating the use of trolleybuses, has also decided that, in future, transport undertakings proposing to discontinue tramway systems shall be free to choose whichever type of vehicle they prefer in substitution.

10 July — The revised fare structure announced in January is introduced.

October — Tramcar 8 is withdrawn after accidental damage.

1 October — Closure of the Balsall Heath, Moseley and Kings Heath group of tram routes, worked from Moseley Road depot: 37 (City-Cannon Hill), 38 (City-Kings Heath via Balsall Heath), 39 City-Alcester Lanes End via Balsall Heath), 40 (City-Kings Heath via Leopold Street), 41 (City-Trafalgar Road via Leopold Street), 42 (City-Alcester Lanes End via Bradford Street), 48 (City-Kings Heath via Bradford Street), 50 (Albert Street-Trafalgar Road via Bradford Street), 65 (City-Moseley Village via Leopold Street), 66 (City-Moseley Village via Balsall Heath) and 67 (City-Moseley Village via Bradford Street). A number of these routes are short workings which had been discontinued before the final abandonment. All of the

above are replaced by bus services 48, 49, 49B and 50 the following day, and Moseley Road depot becomes a bus garage. These closures allow the withdrawal of the 39 remaining cars from the 401 class of 50 four-wheelers acquired in 1912; they are broken up by December 1949. The 11 other cars in the series had been withdrawn in ones and twos between February 1941 and August 1949.

30 October — Quinton bus garage is opened with capacity for 100 buses, although its first allocation is 72 vehicles to work the 3A, 9, 10 and 34 services.

November — Car 604 is the first of the 587 class of 50 bogie cars acquired in 1920 to be withdrawn.

1 November — A petition presented by residents living near to a 'Bundy' time recording clock used by the Transport Department in Pershore Road calls for its removal owing to the noise it makes when in use. Although a more suitable position for the clock cannot be found, crews are instructed to 'carry out their duties as quietly as possible'.

31 December — Closure of 3X (City-Witton via Aston Cross) and 6 (City-Perry Barr) tram routes, which are replaced by bus services 39 and 33 the following day. This allows the last remaining cars from the first batch of 20 purchased to open the Corporation's tramway service in January 1904 to be withdrawn, plus two former City of Birmingham Tramways Co cars, Nos 451 and 452. Ten trams from the 301 class of 100 four-wheelers acquired in 1911 are also withdrawn and broken up between January and February 1950.

Above left: Of the 10 54-seat Crossley HOE7s (Nos 1646-55) delivered in 1949, the last was unusual in having a turbo-transmitter. It was caught in traffic outside Lyons Corner House on Colmore Row on 13 June 1964. *Ron Moss*

Left: It was last in, first out for Daimler CWA6 No 1458, which had a service life of just six years for Birmingham Corporation (1945-50). The vehicle is seen beside car No 339 of 1911 at the Chester Road terminus of Route 79.
  D. R. Harvey Collection

Above: The interior of Quinton bus garage just before its opening on 30 October 1949. At the extreme right is a sunken workshop and a tunnel which interconnected all of the inspection pits. *IAL*

Below: The entrance to Quinton bus garage from Ridgacre Road. Seen on 19 November that year with some of its allocation of 72 buses to work the 3A, 9, 10 and 34 services. *IAL*

Top: On 19 November 1949, six of Quinton's Daimlers undergo servicing over its inspection pits, by the sunken workshop. Nearest to the camera is No 1576 of 1947. *IAL*

Above: The Traffic and Ticket Office at the new Quinton bus garage in April 1950. *IAL*

Above left: A view of the inspection pits from the sunken workshop in the newly completed Quinton bus garage. The passageway at right interconnected those pits not directly abutting the sunken workshop, so that engineering staff did not have to return to floor level to reach it. *IAL*

Above: The 42 tram route (City-Alcester Lanes End via Bradford Street) was one of 10 closed on 1 October 1949. It allowed the withdrawal of the 39 remaining cars from the 401 class of 50 four-wheelers acquired in 1912, which were all broken up by December 1949. On 18 April 1948, No 414 is seen waiting at Alcester Lanes End for No 843 to load and depart. *V. C. Jones/IAL*

Left: The 6 (City-Perry Barr) tram route closed on 31 December 1949, allowing the remaining cars from the first batch of 20 purchased to open the tramway service in January 1904 to be withdrawn. Last of the batch, No 20, is seen working the route in its final months.
D. A. Thompson/Author's collection

Above: On a weekend furlough during his National Service, Mike Waller visited Birmingham on 17 and 18 July 1949. Mostly in heavy rain, he photographed trams on the routes due for closure on 1 October 1949. No 721 is seen at the 37 terminus in Navigation Street. *Mike Waller/TMS*

Below: No 420 on route 42 in High Street. *Mike Waller/TMS*

Top: No 426 on an unusual working of route 50 at Alcester Lanes End. *Mike Waller/TMS*

Above: During his 'wet weekend' in July 1949, Mike Waller also photographed trams on the routes to be closed on 31 December. No 610 is seen on the 3x route at its terminus in Witton. *Mike Waller/TMS*

Above: A view down Hill Street, looking towards
Hurst Street and the tower atop the Hippodrome. Car
No 366 is inbound working the 39 route from Alcester
Lanes End, passing materials piled up ready for road
repairs. The route closed on 1 October 1949 with the
closure of the Moseley services.
Author's collection

Above right: Hill Street, with the former junction with
Station Street to the right. Car No 436 is outbound on
the 41 route to Trafalgar Road, whilst COG5 1213
works inbound from Gospel Lane, and COG5 102
works the 15A service to Yardley.
Author's collection

Right: On 28 June 1949 Daimler COG5 57 pulls
away on the Warstock service 24, leaving car
No 426 working Route 67 and an unidentified car on
Route 39. Both trams were withdrawn with the
closure of the Moseley routes on 2 October 1949,
and 57 was withdrawn in 1950.
W. A. Camwell/National Tramway Museum

The Queen's Hotel towers over car No 432 as it waits to depart Navigation Street, as Leyland PD2 1675 turns right out of Pinfold Street, one day in June 1949. Car and route had four months left to run, but the bus remained in service until 1968.
W. A. Camwell/National Tramway Museum

Above: Car No 420 nudges out of Moseley Road depot, with its trolley pole leading, seeking kicks on a warm day in June 1949 — its last summer.
W. A. Camwell/National Tramway Museum

Above right: An unidentified 401 class car is seen in Moseley depot yard during its last summer. The car and its route, 52, were withdrawn on 2 October 1949.
W. A. Camwell/National Tramway Museum

Right: Car No 408 swings out of Leopold Street into Moseley Road on 28 June 1949 to give chase to Leyland PD2 1660 working service 35 to the Maypole. This service, plus the tram and its route, last ran on 1 October 1949.
W. A. Camwell/National Tramway Museum

Above left: Amidst activity in Witton Square on 10 July 1949, car No 342 was working Route 81 Lozells-Pype Hayes Park. In January 1921 the car was fitted with experimental sheet metal vestibule covers, which it carried until its withdrawal in September 1950. *M. J. O'Connor/National Tramway Museum*

Left: Car No 451 works past Washwood Heath depot to allow car No 13 to run in on 10 July 1949. The depot's routes closed on 30 September 1950. It was a former CBT Co car, acquired in July 1911 with sister car No 452. They were the longest trams operated by the Corporation. *M. J. O'Connor/National Tramway Museum*

Above: The Arcadian Centre has gobbled up most of the buildings in Hurst Street behind car No 445 on Route 41 and car No 427 working Route 37. They were photographed on 1 October 1949, their last day of operation. *W. A. Camwell/National Tramway Museum*

Below: On the last day of operation, car No 432 works Route 40 into Bishop Street from the end of Hurst Street. No-one seems too concerned over what was about to be lost. *W. A. Camwell/National Tramway Museum*

1950: ANOTHER ERA ENDS

As the first of the new design buses was delivered, and the tramway abandonment programme proceeded, the Transport Department suffered a great loss with the sudden death of the General Manager, Mr A. C. Baker, breaking his family's stewardship of the undertaking. The next tramway closure was of the Washwood Heath routes, and one of the trams withdrawn as part of this was set aside for inclusion in the city's new Museum of Science & Industry. At the year's end a new General Manager took up his post. Many of the bus orders were delivered, with 415 new vehicles, comprising 100 Daimler CVD6s with 54-seat Metropolitan-Cammell bodies (2031-130); 50 Leyland PD2s with 56-seat bodies (2131-180); 50 Leyland PD2s with 54-seat bodies by Park Royal (2181-230); 30 Leyland PS2/1s with 34-seat single-deck bodies by Weymann (2231-60); five Leyland Olympics with 32- or 36-seat single-deck bodies by Metropolitan-Cammell (2261-5); 30 Crossley 55-seaters (2396-425); 100 Crossley DD42/7 54-seaters (2426-525) and 50 Guy Arab IV 6LWs with 54-seat bodies by Metropolitan-Cammell (2526-75). Withdrawn buses include: 13 AEC Regents from 1929; 19 from 1930; 13 from 1931; 29 Daimler COG5s from 1935; 23 Daimler COG5s from 1936; 37 Daimler COG5s from 1937; 30 Daimler COG5s from 1938; 32 Leyland TD6cs from 1939; 17 Daimler COG5s from 1939 and seven Leyland TD7cs from 1939.

February — 2426, the first of 100 complete Crossley buses (chassis and bodies) enters service, with the Transport Department's new front styling, featuring the radiator totally enclosed behind a grille, and prominent front service and destination indicators.

31 March — The fleet currently comprises 329 trams, 1,389 buses and 74 trolleybuses, and the Transport Committee's annual report notes that whilst its financial position appears to be healthy, all of its reserves are earmarked for planned expenditure, and the expected revenue is just sufficient to cover known obligations. Two additional costs — increased duty on diesel oil and superannuation on wages — are due to come into effect during the next financial year and are likely to add a further £276,661 to operating costs.

July — The first of the Guy Arab buses are delivered featuring the Transport Department's new front styling.

4 July — In its annual report the Transport Committee notes that an additional £213,068 is required under the 'Rise and Fall' clause in the contracts placed for 335 buses due for delivery in 1948. Costings have also been made for the total cost of reinstating the roadways after the removal of the remaining tram tracks. The total bill for this is likely to be £101,445.

22 July — Arthur Chantrey Baker CBE, General Manager of the Transport Department, dies suddenly at home at the age of 62. He has worked for the Corporation since 1922,

and been General Manager, in succession to his father, since 1928. At the Council meeting held on 25 July, the Lord Mayor pays tribute to Mr Baker's long years of loyal service and expresses his sympathy to his family. The entire Council then honours Mr Baker's memory by standing in silence.

30 September — Closure of the Washwood Heath depot tram routes: 8 (City-Alum Rock), 10 (City-Washwood Heath), and the Witton depot route: 5 (Lozells-Gravelly Hill). These are replaced the following day by bus services 55B and 56, and Washwood Heath and Witton depots become bus garages. This allows the withdrawal of the remaining 26 trams from the 301 class of 100 four-wheelers acquired in 1911; 25 of them are broken up by the end of November 1950, but one, 395, survives following a request from the City Museum & Art Gallery Department that a tramcar should be preserved. It remains at Kyotts Lake Road Works used as a shunter, towing dead bogie cars to Witton depot for breaking up, and is eventually installed in the Museum of Science & Industry in June 1953. The closure of the Lozells route also precipitates the withdrawal of 9 cars from the 512 class of 50 bogie cars

Above left: No 2426, the first of an order for 100 complete Crossley buses, entered service in February 1950. Seen here parked just off Greenwood Avenue, Fox Hollies, it was the first bus in service with the Transport Department's new front styling, featuring a radiator totally enclosed behind a grille, and prominent front route and destination indicators. *Passenger Transport/IAL*

Above: This off-side front three-quarter view of Crossley No 2426, taken on the same date and at the same location, emphasises the radical departure in bus styling which the Birmingham 'new front' represented. *Passenger Transport/IAL*

acquired in 1913, and the closure of Washwood Heath depot also lead to the withdrawal of 26 of the 587 class of 50 bogie cars acquired in 1920.

10 October — Loan sanction for a scheme to erect a bus garage at Lea Hall, revived by the Transport Committee in July 1947, has still not been received, and tenders for the work have to be revised. Originally priced at £175,000, this figure has risen to £215,600, with £180,000 alone being the cost of the building work. The Transport Committee has also been requested to vacate a portion of the city's main Museum & Art Gallery, which they have occupied since the war. Alternative temporary accommodation is offered in the former premises of Messrs Elkington's Ltd in Newhall Street, which has been purchased for the new Museum of Science & Industry. The Committee has until 31 March 1951 to make the move.

7 November — Estimates for the bus requirements for 1952 show that 225 vehicles will be needed. Of these, 114 are required needed following the abandonment of trams on the Bristol and Pershore roads routes; 91 to replace pre-war vehicles and 20 to meet the needs of additional traffic. Provisional costings for these vehicles come to £1,008,000.

9 December — Wilfred Harry Smith is appointed General Manager of the Transport Department, applications having been received from 32 individuals, many of whom were managers of municipal transport undertakings. Mr Smith has worked for the Department since August 1912, when he began as a Junior Clerk. He became Assistant Traffic Superintendent on 1 April 1927, and Traffic Superintendent on 1 February 1942.

Left: Large bus deliveries in 1950 displaced prewar and wartime vehicles, some of which went to W. T. Bird & Sons at Stratford-upon-Avon. Seen there that year, left to right, are No 1336, a Guy Arab I 5LW of 1942; No 195, a Daimler COG5 of 1938 and No 246, a Leyland Titan TD6c of 1939. *D. R. Harvey Collection*

Below left: On 30 March 1950 AEC Regent I No 377 of 1930 is acting as a learner bus at Kyotts Lake Road Works, as fewer numbers of tram crew are required following tramway route abandonments. *Alan B. Cross/D. R. Harvey Collection*

Above: Leyland PS2/1 No 2240, with a 34-seat body by Weymann, was one of a batch of 30 (Nos 2231-60) delivered in 1950 to renew the single-deck fleet. It is seen here on a Special Working outside the Town Hall on 13 June 1964 *Ron Moss*

Below: The lines of the Leyland PS2/1 single-deckers show up well in this view of No 2255 in preservation at Didcot on 18 September 1971. It had worked from its delivery in 1950 until withdrawal in 1969, being disposed of in August 1971. *C. T. Duckitt/IAL*

Above left: The Leyland PS2/1s were used extensively on the 27 service, Kings Heath-West Heath via Northfield, where No 2247 is seen at work. *IAL*

Left: Photographed on 2 November 1950, No 2032 was the second in an order of 100 Daimler CVD6s, with 54-seat Metropolitan-Cammell bodies (Nos 2031-130), delivered that year. It bore the Corporation's revolutionary new front end design. *IAL*

Above: Washwood Heath closed as a tram depot with the cessation of its routes on 30 September 1950. One year earlier, on 4 September 1949, Car 783 working route 10 (City-Washwood Heath) approaches the terminus by the Beaufort cinema, which is showing 'A Letter from Three Wives'.
A.. D. Packer/Author's collection

On 8 August 1949 car No 615 working Route 3X down Park Road, meets car No 347 on Route 60 at Aston Cross. This busy confluence of routes was less busy after the closure of Routes 3, 3X, and 5 on 30 September 1950.
W. A. Camwell/National Tramway Museum

Above: During his weekend furlough in Birmingham, Mike Waller also photographed trams working on routes closed on 30 September 1950. No 808 is seen at the Route 8 terminus at Alum Rock. *Mike Waller/TMS*

Below: There is amazing interest in Chetwyn's window, which allows 587 Class car No 593 to slip out of Navigation Street almost unnoticed on a Route 70 working to Rednal. The tram had but a few months of service left, being broken up in November 1950. *Author's collection*

1951: THE DEATH OF SILENCE

Change was in the air in 1951, no more so than with the Festival of Britain, whose Land Travelling Exhibition was in Bingley Hall, Birmingham, between 4-25 August. Signs of change in the city too, as, with so little tramway left, the Festival was promoted by an illuminated bus. There were no further tramway closures this year, but the nearly 30-year-long 'experiment' with trolleybuses came to an end in June. Behind the scenes, the Transport Department's new General Manager had to face rises in fuel tax and materials costs, precipitating the need for a further fare increase. Another 168 new buses were delivered: 50 Guy Arab IV 6LWs with 54-seat bodies by Metropolitan-Cammell (2576-625) and 118 Daimler CVD6s with 54-seat Metropolitan-Cammell bodies (2626-756). Fifteen vehicles were withdrawn: four Daimler COG5s from 1936; six Daimler COG5s from 1937; one Daimler COG5 from 1938; one Leyland TD6c from 1939, after an accident, and three Daimler COG5s from 1939.

January — Following trials since 1949, the Transport Committee recommends the introduction of a new type of 'Ultimate' ticket issuing machine in place of bell punches. These are phased in from February 1952, the last bell punches being used in July 1954, except on the service to Elmdon Airport, where they survive until January 1963.

9 January — The Transport Committee reports that 314 of its drivers have qualified for awards from the Royal Society for the Prevention of Accidents (RoSPA); these

The new front design buses soon became a familiar sight around the city. In May 1951, Crossley DD42/7 54-seater No 2459 is parked up on the 15B service. It was one of a batch of 100 Crossleys (Nos 2426-525). *G. H. F. Atkins*

become an annual event. It also notes that it has entered into an agreement to purchase and test two lightweight buses which will be delivered in about 18 months' time.

6 February — The Traffic Advisory Committee warns that morning and evening congestion is likely to persist until the Inner Ring Road is constructed. A traffic survey conducted at 33 points in the city centre on 6 July 1950 backs this up. That day, in Corporation Street, near Fore Street, 1,035 vehicles passed between 8.30am and 9.30am.

1 March — Mr Harry Parker, Chief Engineer to the Transport Department is promoted to the post of Deputy General Manager. He has worked for the Department since January 1909.

31 March — The fleet comprises 263 trams, 1,487 buses and 74 trolleybuses, and the Transport Committee's annual report shows a net revenue deficiency of £206,539. Although this is covered by existing assets, these have been earmarked for the rolling programme of tramway and trolleybus replacement reported on 5 July 1949. Added to this, wage awards, fuel tax rises and a continued rise in the cost of materials, are likely to add a further £350,000 to the Department's running costs in the next financial year. A fare increase can therefore not be avoided.

3 May — An illuminated bus tours various parts of the city daily until 17 May in connection with the Festival of Britain celebrations. It is based on 1022, a Daimler COG5 from 1937, and runs from 9.15pm to 11pm.

30 June — Closure of the Coventry Road trolleybus services 94-99. They are replaced the following day by bus services 57B, 58 and 60. The Lode Lane service to the Rover works is taken over by the BMMO, and operated from Station Street.

1 July — The 20 bus service to Weoley Castle is bolstered by the addition of extra Sunday morning buses.

3 July — In its annual report the Transport Department records that its bus requirement for 1953 will be 225 vehicles, of which 110 will be required to replace trams on the Erdington, Tyburn Road and Short Heath routes, 100 will be needed for the normal replacement of older vehicles, and 15 for additional traffic. These new buses have been costed at £1,134,025. An extra £6,750 is also required to secure 2.84 acres of land in Longbridge Lane, West Heath, for the future erection of a bus garage. There is also a growing staff shortage, despite every effort that has been made to recruit suitable labour 'not only in the city, but in other areas, including Eire'.

19 July — A Public Hearing is held into the impending round of fare increases. Its findings are passed to the Minister of Transport, who challenges a central assumption of a 2d minimum fare, and a compromise is reached of raising some fares, but retaining a 1^1/2d single stage fare for the present. The new fare structure comes into effect on 4 November.

9 December — The 55B bus service is extended from the Raven Hotel into the Shard End Estate.

Left: With just over 54 weeks left to run for both the tram and route, car No 806 waits at Rednal on Route 70 on 17 June 1951. Arguably the most missed of the city's tram routes, the long run to Rednal closed on 5 July 1952, No 806 being broken up at Witton depot the following month. *V. C. Jones/IAL*

Above left: With its impending closure, Birmingham's limited trolleybus system became of even more interest to enthusiasts. Here a party pause for a photo stop during a special tour aboard top-of-the-fleet No 90 in the closing months. *W. J. Haynes/IAL*

Left: On 17 June 1951, 13 days before the closure of the Coventry Road trolleybus services 94-99, six-wheeled Leyland TTBD2 No 50 rounds the corner from Carrs Lane en route to Sheldon. Regarded as a long-term experiment, trolleybus operation was a sideline for Birmingham Corporation. *V. C. Jones/IAL*

Right: One of the last 50 prewar buses delivered to Birmingham Corporation in 1939, Leyland TD6c 52-seater No 1298 waits in Station Street in 1951 to work the 36 service to Stechford. Considered to be amongst the most elegant of the prewar designs, the bus was withdrawn in 1952. *B. W. Ware/ D. R. Harvey Collection*

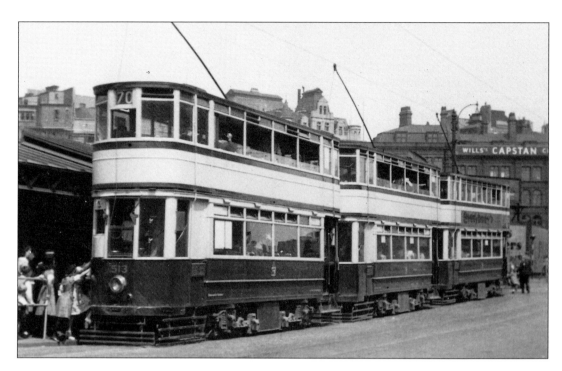

Top: Car No 513 of 1913 brings up the rear of a line of three cars loading up in Navigation Street to work the Bristol Road routes. When these closed in July 1952 No 513 was the oldest car left in the city's fleet. *Author's collection*

Above: An anxious Inspector looks towards the photographer as No 843 waits to depart from Martineau Street on a Special working as No 657 works Route 6 behind. Martineau Street was obliterated in the city's redevelopment in the 1960s. *R. B. Parr/National Tramway Museum*

1952: SHOWCASE CLOSURES

Providing Birmingham's public transport cost the Corporation more than it raised in revenue in 1951/2, denting reserves. The city also bade farewell to its former showcase tramway routes along the Bristol Road, with its long lengths of reserved track. These worked to Rednal (for the Lickey Hills) and Rubery. Despite a growing staff shortage, Trades Union pressure to employ part-time women bus drivers was resisted. Fuel and wage costs continued to rise, and more fare increases were proposed. Just 111 new buses were delivered: 19 Daimler CVD6s with 54-seat bodies by Metropolitan-Cammell (2757-75) and 91 Daimler CVG6s with 55-seat Crossley bodies (2776-858, 2861-8). There was also a Guy Arab, with a Gardner 5LW engine and Saunders-Roe (Anglesey) Ltd-55-seat lightweight body incorporating the Corporation's new front design (3001). Unveiled in December, the construction was all aluminium, with timber floors, and weighed 15 cwt (22.4%) lighter than the equivalent standard body. These allowed 97 older vehicles to be withdrawn: eight Daimler COG5s from 1936; 19 Daimler COG5s from 1937; 11 Daimler COG5s from 1938; 21 Leyland TD6cs from 1939; 19 Daimler COG5s from 1939 and 19 Leyland TD7cs from 1939.

January — Experimental lightweight tram 843 develops motor failure and is withdrawn from service. With non-standard GEC motors, it is not considered worthy of repair, and the car's bodywork is also in poor condition. It is stored at Kyotts Lake Road Works until July and then moved to Witton depot to be broken up, with the other experimental lightweight car, No 842, in August 1952.

8 January — The Council pays tribute to Harry Parker, Deputy General Manager and Chief Engineer of the Transport Department, who has died. His position as Chief Engineer is filled by Mr William Goodall Copestake, the Assistant Chief Engineer, who has worked for the Department since 1930 after engineering experience with the LMS and the Lanchester Motor Co. The post of Deputy General Manager is not filled.

31 March — The vehicle fleet comprises 256 trams and 1,663 buses. The accounts for 1951/2 show an operating deficiency on the tram, bus and trolleybus services amounting to £621,916. This is reduced when certain adjustments are made, but requires the transfer of funds from the City Treasurer to cover it, and further diminishes the Department's reserves.

Guy Arab No 3001 had a 55-seat lightweight body by Saunders-Roe (Anglesey) Ltd. Unveiled in December 1953, it incorporated the Corporation's new front design. The construction was all aluminium, with timber floors, and weighed 15cwt (22.4%) lighter than the equivalent standard body. *Passenger Transport/IAL*

April — Car No 814, of the 30-strong batch of air-brake bogie cars (Nos 812-841) acquired in 1928, is struck by lightning whilst stationary in Bristol Street near Bromsgrove Street. It catches fire and five people have to be treated for burns.

June — More 'Bundy' clock problems. A petition presented to this month's Council meeting complains about the noise resulting from buses using a time clock in Monument Road. Upon investigation the complaint is upheld and the clock is moved towards the Ledsham Street end of the railway bridge in Monument Road.

5 July — Closure of the Bristol Road tram routes: 35 (City-Selly Oak), 54 (City-Priory Road), 69 (City-Northfield), 70 (City-Rednal), 71 (City-Rubery) and 72 (City-Longbridge), worked from Selly Oak depot, and the Pershore Road tram routes: 36 (City-Cotteridge), 46 (City-British Oak) and 53 (City-Dogpool), worked from Cotteridge depot. These are replaced by bus services 61, 62, 63 and 45 the following day, when Cotteridge and Selly Oak depots become bus garages. The 61 bus service is also introduced to serve the Allens Cross Estate at Northfield. Amongst the trams withdrawn as a result of this is car No 341, the last of the 301 class of 100 four-wheelers acquired in 1911. In 1945 it served as the 'Victory' illuminated tram, and had then been converted to a single-deck supply car, serving out its time at Selly Oak. This closure also occasions the withdrawal of:

• 19 cars from the 512 class of 50 bogie cars acquired in 1913, broken up at Witton depot by the end of August;

Left: Some of the secrets of No 3001's light weight are revealed in this maker's shot of the body under construction. Much weight was saved on the intermediate floor unit, the aluminium pressings of which carried floor loads to the main body pillars. *Passenger Transport/IAL*

Below left: Inside the lower saloon of lightweight-bodied Guy Arab No 3001 of December 1952. *Passenger Transport/IAL*

Above: Work to convert Cotteridge depot into a bus garage was under way before closure of the Pershore Road routes on 5 July 1952. Here cars Nos 820, 816 and 810 eye the building work with suspicion. *Photomatic Ltd/Author's collection*

Below: With less than a month to go before its conversion into a bus garage, the reworking of Selly Oak depot is in full swing on 7 June 1952. Car No 750 is in the foreground, but most interest surrounds lightweight car No 842.
Pamlin Prints/Author's collection

Above: Also lost on 5 July 1952 — the date of closure of a number or tramway routes — were scenes like these: No 513 on Route 70 on the reserved track along the Bristol Road… *Lacey's Studios/Author's collection*

Below: …and No 772 on Route 70 at Rednal on 8 June 1952. *Pamlin Prints/Author's collection*

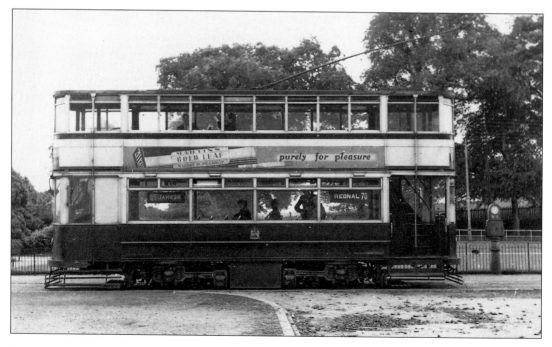

• the remaining 22 trams, from the first batch of 30 air-brake cars (732-61) acquired by the Department in 1926, broken up at Witton depot by the end of August;
• the 49 cars in the second batch of 50 air-brake bogie cars (762-811) acquired in 1928; and,
• the 26 cars remaining from the 30-strong batch of air-brake bogie cars (812-41) also acquired in 1928.

12 August — Arising from a suggestion made at the Council Meeting on 29 July that the Department employ part-time women bus drivers, a meeting is held with representatives of the Transport & General Workers' Union (TGWU), but it is decided that there being no shortage of men 'the employment of part-time women drivers is undesirable'.

28 September — Budget fuel tax and wage increases necessitate a further round of fare increases, introduced today. These had been discussed at a public hearing held on 16 July, and were approved by the Minister of Transport on 20 August. Increases are across the range of fares, and the 2d minimum, sought earlier, becomes a reality. The minimum Workmen's Return rises to 10d, and the All-Night basic flat fare rises 2d to 8d.

30 November — Over the last 12 months, 34 bus shelters have been erected using funds from the A. W. Keep Bequest. The Department has also devised a programme to continue this work over the next two years.

Left: On 5 July 1952 car No 559 works down Chapel Lane to Selly Oak on its last day as a tram depot. The car was reallocated to Miller Street depot and saw out the end of Birmingham's tramways in July 1953.
Robert F. Mack/Author's collection

Below: The premises of the Birmingham Battery Metal Co Ltd form an appropriately electrical backdrop to car No 561 on the depot approach at Selly Oak on 5 July 1952. Serving out its time at Miller Street, No 561 was broken up at Kyotts Lake Road in July 1953, whilst the backdrop is now 'Battery Park' retail park. *Photomatic Ltd/Author's collection*

Left: Motorists who had become accustomed to trams crossing from Rednal terminus to Lickey Road, as car No 765 has just done, had unfamiliar freedom on 6 July 1952, when buses took over their duties. The tram survived only one month, being broken up in Witton depot that August.
L. L. Jones/Author's collection

Below: Closure of the Bristol Road tram routes on 5 July 1952 allowed 19 cars from the 512 class of 50 bogie cars acquired in 1913 to be withdrawn. Class leader No 512 is seen rounding the curve from Navigation Street into John Bright Street on Route 35 (City-Selly Oak), one of those to close.
L. L. Jones/Author's collection

Right: A passenger prepares to step off car No 577 as it works one of Birmingham's three remaining tram routes, stopping inbound on Route 2 at Aston Cross, 7 June 1952.
J. H. Meredith/Author's collection

Below right: The top decks of the trams withdrawn and scrapped with the closure of the Bristol and Pershore roads routes are seen in the yard of W. T. Bird & Sons at Stratford-upon-Avon on 16 July 1952. *D. R. Harvey Collection*

Bottom right: Old Tom, the University clock, says 10.17 as No 528 loads and unloads at Edgbaston Park Road on a bright sunny day in 1952. Despite the permanence of the scene, both tram and route had but weeks to go.
R. Knibbs/National Tramway Museum

1953: A LITTLE SOMETHING ON THE SIDE

Although Birmingham's trams had long carried advertisements on both their fronts and sides, the city's buses had been unsullied by such commercialism. It was therefore some outward measure of the financial straits in which the Transport Department found itself that advertisements began to appear on the buses at the start of the year. After several attempts, a free travel scheme for the city's old age pensioners was introduced in May, but if they wanted to use them on the Corporation's trams they had just two months to do so before the last trams ran in July. Later in the year permission was given to begin the reconstruction of Digbeth and Deritend, something only made possible by an earlier tramway abandonment. Deliveries of another 184 new buses began, continuing into 1954: 84 Daimler CVG6s with 55-seat Crossley bodies (2869-900, 3103-53); and 100 Guy Arab IV 6LWs with 55-seat bodies by Metropolitan-Cammell (3003-102). One of the Daimlers (3103) was an experimental lightweight vehicle with a body weighing 2 tons 12cwt, a saving of 15cwt (22.4%) over the equivalent standard body. With many of the older buses already withdrawn, just 25 left service: two Daimler COG5s from 1936, and 23 Daimler COG5s from 1937.

6 January — Spiralling wage costs bring a pessimistic forecast for the Department's end of year accounts, and new ways are sought to raise revenue. One source was through allowing advertising on buses. Up to this point the presence of advertisements on buses had been thought to be 'most undesirable from the æsthetic point of view', but rising operating costs change minds on the subject. Tenders have been sought, and that of Frank Mason & Co

Left: How better to report the first use of advertisements on the Corporation buses than to show one of your own being applied? So thought the *Evening Despatch* when it ran this picture on 31 January 1953. Advertisements had been carried on the buses since 1 January. Guy Arab IV No 3000 was the only one of its batch to carry a 'LOG' registration number. *Birmingham Gazette & Despatch/IAL*

Below right: No 2880, a Daimler CVG6 of 1953 with a 55-seat Crossley body, is seen on the 13A service in Colmore Row, just past the junction with Waterloo Street. It was one of 184 new buses delivered to the Corporation that year and carried advertisements from new. *Ron Moss*

of London is accepted for five years. Under the arrangement, Mason's let space on the exterior upper sides and lower rear panels, the Department receiving 70% of the gross annual receipts from this, and 75% of these if they exceed £91,000. In the first year this arrangement is forecast to bring in £47,187, £56,964 in the second and fifth years, and £58,984 in the remainder. The first buses bearing advertisements appear on the streets on 1 January.

31 March — The Transport Department's fleet comprises 120 trams and 1,786 buses. The accounts for 1952/3 show a revenue deficiency of £331,799 which, when added to the deficiency brought forward from the previous year, makes a total of £722,107. A relaxation of an obligation upon the Department to make good such deficiencies during the year after they arise, made by the Minister of Transport, is therefore welcomed, but these cannot roll forward for more than five years, so a need to do something to rectify the situation is recognised.

3 May — Free travel passes are introduced for 'aged persons' in receipt of either a retirement or old age pension or National Assistance. By 19 June 33,689 such passes have been issued, and by 30 November the number is up to 40,070.

June — Car No 395, from the 301 class of 100 four-wheelers acquired in 1911, is delivered to and assembled in the Birmingham Museum of Science & Industry.

29 June — A Public Hearing is held over the Transport Department's proposals to withdraw or amend those bus services it considers to be unprofitable. Overall, it is proposed to withdraw all cross-city services, and to substitute two services with suitable interchange points in the city centre. Modifications are proposed to the 5A/7, 15A/16A, 19, 29, 29A, 33/34 and 36 routes, and the 46 and 57B are

proposed for withdrawal. Implementation of these changes is subject to approval by the Licensing Authority for Public Service Vehicles, to whom application has been made.

1 July — One consequence of the impending abandonment of tramway services is the ending of Police responsibility for dealing with items of lost property found on tramcars and in taxicabs. As a result, a new Lost Property Section has been established from this date at Miller Street depot.

4 July — Closure of the 1 (City-Stockland Green), 2 (City-Erdington), 63 (City-Tyburn Road), 64 (City-High Street, Erdington), 78 (City-Short Heath) and 79 (City-Pype Hayes Park) — the last in the city. They are replaced the same day by bus services 65, 66 and 64, and Miller Street depot also becomes a bus garage. A total of £68,757 has been spent on the conversion of Miller Street, Washwood Heath, Coventry Road, Selly Oak and Cotteridge depots to bus garages.

The closing of Birmingham's tramway is a somewhat subdued affair. The tracks of the remaining routes come together for a common approach to the city along Lichfield Road, and it is decided to withdraw trams from service by stopping them at the junction with Victoria Road, Aston, and transferring their passengers to buses. This process begins around 10.30am, and the withdrawn trams are then driven to Witton depot, via Victoria Road, Park Road and Witton Lane. An exception is made for the last trams on each service, which return to their operating depot at Miller Street; the last ones into the depot are the official last cars, Nos 616 and 623, both on Route 2. Car No 616 is daubed, graffiti-style, in white paint with the slogans 'BIRMINGHAM'S LAST TRAMCAR' along each side, below the lower saloon windows, and with the words 'THE END' on each dash panel. Criticised as being 'amateurish', few realise that this paint scheme has been tried a week or so earlier on withdrawn car No 710 in Kyotts Lake Road Works. Also, howsoever crudely executed, it is noticeable that the City Coat of Arms sits neatly in between the 's' of 'Birmingham'S' and the 'L' of 'Last', and that the fleet number similarly sits squarely between 'THE' and 'END' on each dash. That evening the majority of the trams remaining in Miller Street depot are driven to Kyotts Lake Road in convoy, beginning at 6pm. They face one problem: in Carrs Lane, the link between High Street and Moor Street, the overhead has been removed, so the trams have to coast down to Moor Street where they regain the overhead. Any that fail to make it round into Moor Street are given a friendly nudge by breakdown lorry No 15, converted from a 1931 AEC Renown double-decker. From there they go via Digbeth, Rea and Bradford streets to the Stratford Road and Kyotts Lake Road Works, the last in being 679.

As a result of the closure of the tramway service, all of the remaining trams are withdrawn and broken up at Kyotts Lake Road Works in August 1953:

- 31 cars from the 512 class of 50 bogie cars acquired in 1913, 586 the last to be broken up;
- 15 cars from the 587 class of 50 bogie cars acquired in 1920, including 616, the official last tram, 634 being the last to be broken up;
- 20 cars from the 637 class of 25 bogie cars acquired in 1923, 660 being the last to be broken up; and,
- 14 cars from the 702 class of 30 bogie cars acquired in 1925, 728 being the last to be broken up.

The final abandonment of tramway operation in the city leaves many tons of tram rails set in the streets. This year the Transport Department is due to remove 2,000 tons of rails, with an estimated value of £6 per ton. However, an approach from the Iron & Steel Federation (ISF) to take up these rails, and to pay £12 per ton for them, is accepted. This is made on the condition that the Corporation subsequently removes a further 6,000 tons of rails within nine months, for which the ISF will also pay £12 per ton. In this way the majority of the tram rails will be removed from the city's streets at a relatively small cost to the Corporation. The remaining overhead and poles in the city have been purchased by W. T. Bird & Sons of Stratford-upon-Avon for £31,800.

5 July — Employees of W. T. Bird & Sons begin work to remove the overhead wires on the Aston-Erdington route.

7 July — The breaking up of trams is under way at Witton and the last eight cars stored in Miller Street depot are moved there under their own power. The last car in is No 623 of 1920, which enters the depot at around 8.15pm.

7 July — For the first time since its inception the Transport Committee delivers an annual report only as a bus operator. It is therefore thought timely to reflect upon the contribution the Transport undertaking has made to the growth of the city: 'Not only has it provided cheap and efficient services for the citizens of Birmingham and developed such services to cover the whole of the city's area, but it has been the means, by reason of its development, to enable the city itself to develop. The many housing estates which have been built during the past thirty years would have failed in their usefulness but for the fact that transport services have been made available for the use of the residents.' In a direct way too, the undertaking, and principally the tramways, have made a substantial financial contribution to the city coffers. Figures are reported for the years 1904-53 which include:

- Annual contributions to the rates £790,580
- Road maintenance and construction £2,377,525
- Street widening £399,374
- Rates on tram track and buildings £2,894,302

Overall, the Transport Department has contributed £6,966,333 to the city's revenue to date, and this sum exceeds its outstanding loans by £2,227,359. These figures include an liability for the reinstatement of road following the removal of tram track, for which the sum of £376,791 has been allowed.

Initial trials with advertising on buses have been so successful that this is to be extended to the rear panels of single-deck vehicles, and to upper rear panels of double-deck ones, plus the interior bulkheads of both types. This will increase the annual advertising revenue by £18,750.

17 July — By 10am tram 616, Birmingham's official last tram, has been scrapped at Witton depot

24/25 July — The first of two sales of tramway items at Witton depot by W. T. Bird & Sons of Stratford-on-Avon; the second is held in August.

30 July — The Minister of Transport announces that Birmingham can proceed immediately with a £240,000 scheme for the reconstruction and widening of Digbeth and Deritend. Permission had been sought for this scheme since 1951, and it had its origins in the early 1930s, when concern grew at the traffic congestion in these areas. The first properties were acquired by compulsory purchase under the Corporation's Act of 1935.

6 August — The last of the trams, No 597 of 1920, is broken up at Kyotts Lake Road Works. Permanent Way car PW8 also makes the last movement under power by a Birmingham tram when it is moved into the road for a final group photograph.

14/15 August — W. T. Bird & Sons of Stratford-on-Avon holds a further sale of tram fittings at Witton depot, including seats, plate glass and doors.

13 September — A revised fare structure is introduced under which most fares stay the same, but are reduced by one fare stage in the distance they cover. These changes are forecast to increase revenue by £318,758. The proposed changes to unremunerative services announced in June are, however, dropped following their rejection by the Licensing Authority for Public Service Vehicles.

4 JULY 1953 — THE LAST DAY OF TRAMWAY OPERATION

A large crowd gathered in Steelhouse Lane to see Birmingham's official last tram, No 616, depart on the morning of 4 July 1953. Viewed from the roof of the Gaumont cinema, the tram prepares to depart. It would survive for just 13 more days, but within 15 years everything else in this scene would also be swept away. *Birmingham Post & Mail/IAL*

Above: Only the crowds along the road and on the balconies of the General Hospital tell that this is the last day working of Route 2 as No 690 heads for Erdington at 10.45 on 4 July 1953. *R. Knibbs/National Tramway Museum*

Left: After 10.30am on 4 July 1953 inbound cars, such as No 713, were stopped at the junction of Lichfield Road with Victoria Road for the transfer of passengers to waiting buses, such as Guy 3203 on tram replacement service 64. *R. Knibbs/National Tramway Museum*

Below left: At 11.58 on 4 July 1953, No 616 enters Miller Street depot and performs the final passenger carrying duty of a Birmingham tram, ending 49 years of Corporation tramway operation. *R. Knibbs/National Tramway Museum*

Above right: Official last tram No 616 passes No 623 on 4 July 1953, the last morning of tramway operation in Birmingham. *Lacey's Studios/National Tramway Museum*

Right: From 6.30pm on 4 July 1953 24 trams were moved from Miller Street depot to Kyotts Lake Road works, through the city centre. Here car No 650 is seen in High Street, beginning its descent of Carrs Lane, from which the overhead wires had been removed. *R. J. S. Wiseman/National Tramway Museum*

Left: The withdrawn trams moved down Carrs Lane under gravity, as No 722 shows. *R. J. S. Wiseman/ National Tramway Museum*

Below left: The most difficult part of the coast down Carrs Lane was the curve into Moor Street at the bottom. Car 546 makes it with ease, but 586 became stuck here and required a push from a breakdown lorry. *R. J. S. Wiseman/ National Tramway Museum*

Below: From Moor Street the transferring trams entered the Bull Ring, as No 548 has just done in this view which is completely unrecognisable today. *R. J. S. Wiseman/ National Tramway Museum*

Right: From the Bull Ring the trams moved down Digbeth, dislodging dirt from these seldom-used tracks. *R. J. S. Wiseman/ National Tramway Museum*

Below right: The last car into Kyotts Lake Road works on the evening of 4 July 1953 was No 679, which is seen entering the works without ceremony. *R. J. S. Wiseman/ National Tramway Museum*

Above: On Thursday 6 August 1953 Permanent Way Car 8 enjoyed the dubious distinction of being the only scrap tram to leave Kyotts Lake works intact; but this was only to W. T. Bird's scrapyard. As it left, the slogan: '*THIS IS THE END; FAREWELL TO BHAM; SHE'S BEEN A GOOD-UN; THE LOT*' was chalked on the side.
W. A. Camwell/ National Tramway Museum

Right: July 1953: The track at Short Heath terminus has been loosened ready for removal for scrap, and the overhead wire has already gone.
R. Knibbs/National Tramway Museum

Left: The final bill for reinstating the road after removing the tram lines came to over £100,000. As Crossley No 2289 works service 64, the replacement for tram Route 2, on 12 August 1953 the lines last used on 4 July remain in place. *IAL*

Below: Birmingham Corporation's Tyburn Road Works looked more like a factory than a service facility. This overhead crane's-eye view was taken on 14 November 1953 and shows the rear and front axle areas in the foreground, with the gearbox, engine and body areas beyond. Opened on 4 December 1929, the works could undertake the complete rebuilding of buses. *Passenger Transport/IAL*

Almost as soon as Birmingham Corporation's Transport Department achieved a system which could operate wherever there were suitable roads, its Public Works Department embarked upon the first of the major road and redevelopment schemes which would form many people's abiding memories of that city from the late 1950s to the 1970s. None the less, the bus reigned supreme, and the last assets of the tramway system were disposed of in 1954. The much delayed Lea Hall garage opened the following year, but some nostalgia must have lingered for the trams, for a north-south Rapid Transit scheme was proposed in 1956, but, like the underground scheme six years earlier, it was defeated on cost. That same year 'Suez' became a familiar place-name and the fuel rationing which followed the crisis added to the Transport Department's financial woes. Recruitment from amongst Birmingham's ethnic minorities eased the staff shortages, but these were still acute and peak services rarely ran to strength. A decline in passenger numbers began, then accelerated, the blame being laid on

commercial television, motor scooters, or anything; but bus travel conferred no advantage in congested city streets, some of which were being ploughed up for the Inner Ring Road scheme. One answer was a Limited Stop bus service, but it didn't matter how rarely this stopped, when it could hardly get going.

1954: THE 'LAKE' RUNS DRY

Ever since the end of the war, when not all of the Transport Department's employees who had been on active service returned to their jobs, there had been a staff shortage. Over the years this had grown ever more acute, despite recruitment campaigns first nationally, and then in Eire. This year the Department turned its attention to the city's growing ethnic minority populations, from whom many loyal employees were recruited. A strong link with the tram era was also severed with the closure of Kyotts Lake Road Works, its work done. The buses delivered included Guy Arab IV 6LW 3017, with a 55-seat body by Metropolitan-Cammell, this being the 1,000th bus body made for the Transport Department by

PW.1167.

Metropolitan-Cammell since December 1930. In all, 114 new buses were delivered: 74 Daimler CVG6s with 55-seat Crossley bodies (3154-227) and 39 Guy Arab IV 6LWs (3064-102), with 172 older vehicles withdrawn: 10 Daimler COG5s from 1936; 41 Daimler COG5s from 1937; 27 Daimler COG5s from 1938; 17 Leyland TD6cs from 1939; 67 Daimler COG5s from 1939 and 10 Leyland TD7cs from 1939.

5 January — The City Council passes a resolution that 'as it seemed impracticable for many years to construct the Inner Ring Road and other city centre improvements' the Committees of the Council should confer to review all aspects of the traffic problem and to make suggestions for its alleviation. Reporting on the success of letting of advertising on buses, the Transport Committee states that it is proposed to extend this to the front bulkhead of the upper saloon on double-deck vehicles. This is possible on 1,663 such vehicles and will bring in an additional £4,000 per year.

16 March — Staff shortages still trouble the Department. It has tried advertising in Eire, and now the General Manager is authorised to engage any suitable 'coloured labour'. The first such person engaged by the Department as a prospective conductor commences training on 22 March, and by the end of November a total of 379 coloured workers have been engaged, of whom 283 (212 men; 71 women) remain as conductors, 15 have been trained as drivers, and 81 are in the course of instruction.

25 March — A new lease is taken of land formerly occupied by the Permanent Way Yard at Miller Street. The land belongs to the Governors of King Edward VI Grammar Schools and the lease is for 99 years, at £200 per annum, on condition that work commences on the erection of a new bus garage there within five years.

31 March — The Transport Department's fleet comprises 1,834 buses. In its annual report for 1952/3 the Department shows a revenue surplus of £167,493, but it still has an accumulated deficit of £554,614. Ahead loom both wage and pay scale increases, which seem likely to knock out any surplus which may be made. The end of year figures inevitably also contain many items relating to the final abandonment of tramway operation. Replacement buses cost £943,758 and the tramway assets written off total £900,786. The sale of trams for scrapping, to W. T. Bird & Sons of Stratford-upon-Avon, raises £18,178; the sale of tramway equipment a further £5,121 and the sale of machinery and plant £3,368. It is noted that redundant vehicle, overhead and permanent way stores have been disposed of, and sums spent converting facilities to bus operation include £61,611 for road reinstatement and £1,024 in altering Rednal terminus for buses.

April — Kyotts Lake Road Works, the most tramway-dedicated of the Transport Department's facilities, closes. Its last duties have been the breaking up of part of the tramway fleet, work which lasted until 6 August 1953. It had opened in February 1885 for the repair of steam trams operated by the Birmingham Central Tramways Co, and was taken over by the Corporation's Tramways Department from June 1906.

1 May — Deliveries of the Guy Arab IV 6LW buses have reached 3087, and of the Daimlers CVG6s 3183.

30 September — Despite the pessimistic forecasts six months earlier, the half-year figures show that a gross profit in excess of £900,000 is expected on the year, from which a drivers' and conductors' pay award of 8s per week and a new overtime rate of time-and-a-quarter for work on Saturdays after 1pm must come. Allowing for these, a net surplus is still predicted.

1 October — A Daimler CLG5 (3002), with a 55-seat lightweight 'Orion' body by Metropolitan-Cammell incorporating the new front design, enters service. At 2 tons 11cwt, this body is 23.4% lighter than the standard one produced by the company for the Corporation; it is said to offer an 11% fuel saving, amounting to £60 per year.

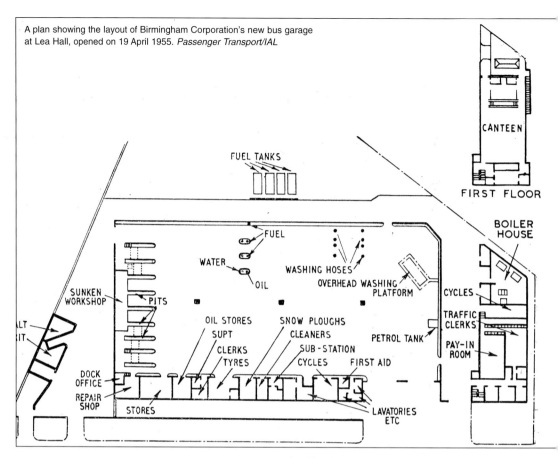

A plan showing the layout of Birmingham Corporation's new bus garage at Lea Hall, opened on 19 April 1955. *Passenger Transport/IAL*

1955: No Accounting for Trams

The Transport Department gained a new garage at Lea Hall and potentially, brighter streets, as the Public Works Committee decided to abandon its high pressure gas street lighting system, installed within the city centre and inaugurated on 10 November 1934. Each 26ft-high lamp contained six mantles and gave 3,000 candle power, but agreement could not be reached with the West Midlands Gas Board over payment, so conversion to electricity was chosen. The year also saw the sale of the last tramway assets and the opening of the new Digbeth/Deritend road scheme, but the most pressing concern was still the staff shortages, which were now having a major impact upon service delivery. No new buses were delivered this year, and only 27 older ones were withdrawn: Daimler COG5 from 1936; five Daimler COG5s from 1937; one Daimler COG5 from 1938; nine Daimler COG5s from 1939 and 11 Leyland TD7cs from 1939-77.

31 March — The Transport Committee's end of year accounts for 1954/5 show a revenue surplus of £164,177. Among the figures included is £75,000 for the transfer value of the former tramway works at Kyotts Lake Road, which closed in April 1954. A further £510 has been raised by the sale of tramway equipment. This is the last time that tramway items will be mentioned in these accounts. The

bus fleet is reported as 1,822 vehicles.

19 April — The Lord Mayor officially opens Lea Hall garage at the corner of Crossfield Road and Kitts Green Road. It stands on a 3.5-acre site and has a capacity for 120 buses. The main garage is 159ft by 345ft, offering 54,855sq ft of uninterrupted floor space; a separate two-storey administration block and canteen has a floor area of 7,488sq ft. Services worked from Lea Hall are the 14 (City-Tile Cross) and part of the 28 (City-Great Barr via Small Heath and Pype Hayes). The opening of Lea Hall garage permits the closure of Barford Street garage, which the Department still has on lease until 25 March 2020. It is transferred to the control of the General Purposes Committee on the receipt of £31,000.

12 June — A revised fare structure is introduced, with increases of 1d for ordinary fares on journeys covering 5, 8 and 11 fare stages, and similar changes to children's and workmen's fares.

12 July — A programme of new bus shelter installation is announced. It covers 55 new shelters over the next 3 years.

22 July — A widened Digbeth and Deritend road system is formally opened by the Minister of Transport.

1 August — The vacant post of Deputy General Manager is filled by the Chief Engineer, Mr William Goodall Copestake, who has worked for the Department

since 1930.

15 August — A bad day for the Transport Department: owing to staff shortages 193 buses remain in their garages and 103 are late out.

1956: TRAMS TO RETURN?

A delegation from the Public Works Committee had visited the USA to study traffic control methods. One of their recommendations was for an electric railway to run between Rubery, in the south of Birmingham, to Eachelhurst Road, on the city boundary in the north at Sutton Coldfield. This was to be based upon Rapid Transit principles as seen in Philadelphia. A 14-mile line was planned,

Above left and left: Two views of Lea Hall bus garage. The left one shows the main 159ft x 345ft garage, with its 54,855sq ft of uninterrupted floor space, whilst the right one shows the sunken workshop and inspection pits. Standing on a 3.5-acre site, the garage had a capacity for 120 buses. Services worked from Lea Hall were the 14 (City-Tile Cross) and part of the 28 (City-Great Barr via Small Heath and Pype Hayes). *Transport World/IAL*

Below: Birmingham Corporation began a regular bus service to Elmdon Airport in 1949, from a newly established air terminal in the city. In June 1956, Leyland Olympic No 2261 (*left*) and Leyland PS2 No 2235 (*right*), both built in 1950, were working the service, which was the last to retain bell punch ticketing. *J. W. Taylor/IAL*

using a combination of central reservation and subway track, which it was estimated would permit a 32.5min end-to-end journey — a favourable comparison with the 59min taken by the buses and the 73min taken by the former trams. Overall the scheme was costed at £9,556,889, but at an average fare of 4d, the scheme was likely to make an annual loss of £360,559, and the break-even average fare of 5³/4d was thought to be too high. Once again, an imaginative public transport scheme was abandoned. No new buses were delivered, or old ones withdrawn, and the Suez crisis brought its own problems by the year's end.

10 January — The Transport Committee reports that a shortage of staff is still causing the Department great concern. Recruitment continues through Labour Exchanges and advertisements, but the net result is that it is not always possible to operate buses to schedule.

31 March — The Transport Department's fleet comprises 1,822 buses. Its end of year figures for 1955/6 show that both operating mileage and passenger figures are down, and its is noted that 'but for the operation of the Aged Persons Free Travel Scheme, a much higher total would have been recorded'. There is a net revenue surplus of £118,233, and carried forward deficiencies have been reduced to below the value of reserves, resulting in an overall surplus of £47,446.

June — With an eye to future orders, AEC loan a Regent V double-decker, with a Park Royal body, to the Corporation for trials. It is worked mainly on the 14 service around Kitts Green and Tile Cross.

1 July — The provisions of the City of Birmingham (Smokeless Area) (No 1) Order 1955 come into effect, banning the use of open coal fires in buildings in part of the city. These have been a major contributor to 'smog', smoke-rich fogs which descended on cities in the winter months and caused traffic hazards.

3 July — Staff problems have eased through recent recruitment, but the Transport Committee reports that there is still an acute shortage of drivers, partly as a result of the need to train newly recruited staff.

August — A revised fare structure is introduced, with across the board ¹/2d increases in the lower 2d and 4d fares, and a 1d rise in the All-Night bus flat fare to 10d.

19 August — *The Birmingham Post & Gazette*, which has been fulminating about the relative profitability of individual bus services, publishes a list showing the receipts per mile of each service. The most profitable is the Inner Circle (8) at 47.04d per mile, and the least profitable the Stechford service (36) at 29.7d per mile.

23 December — In response to fuel rationing resulting from the Suez crisis, a surcharge is added to bus fares.

1957: 'THE INCREASING POPULARITY OF TELEVISION'

Birmingham still had a Victorian city centre, and the rise in the number of motor vehicles had seen traffic increase in parts of the city by over 40% since 1950. Work began on the Inner Ring Road, which many believed to be the solution, but this created its own problems on the way. Passenger numbers were also down, and many thought the two not unconnected, although the blame was well scattered. This, and Suez, helped to create a deficit in 1956/7. Only one new bus was delivered, an AEC Bridgemaster (3,228) with a 72-seat Crossley body, which was on trial.

8 January — Commenting upon the continuing decline in passenger numbers, the Transport Committee identifies a number of factors: 'the recession and consequent strikes and short-time working in the motor car and allied industries, the extension of the five-day working week to many undertakings, including Government and Local Government offices, the changed travel habits of the pub-

Left: In June 1956, AEC loaned a Regent V double-decker with a Park Royal body to the Corporation for trials, with a view to future orders. It was worked mainly on the 14 service in Kitts Green and Tile Cross. *A. A. Cooper/IAL*

Below: Looking around for things to blame for declining passenger numbers, the Transport Committee pointed the finger at scooters, bubblecars, cars in general, the five-day week and television. As 1948-9 Daimler CVG6 No 1872 runs through Icknield Street it passes Jeanne's, who has had trouble with parking, and John James, then a large electrical and television dealer. *Ron Moss*

lic due to television, and the bad weather which has been experienced during the past summer, especially at weekends'.

18 January — Approval is given by the Minister of Transport for the first phase of the Inner Ring Road scheme to commence, the section between Horsefair and the entrance to New Street station. The Minister inaugurates the scheme personally on 8 March 1957 by detonating a charge to demolish a wall, showering everyone with debris and injuring a reporter.

7 March — The Conference of Midland Transport Undertakings is held in Birmingham and chaired by the Chairman of the Transport Committee. Those present pledge to work together to ease the problems associated with the duplication of services, traffic congestion, lack of co-operation and poor liaison with British Railways.

31 March — The Transport Department's fleet again comprises 1,822 buses. Operating mileage and passenger numbers continue to decline. In addition to the reasons for this cited in January, the Transport Committee also considers the 'increase in the number of private cars and motor-assisted vehicles' to be a significant factor. The Suez crisis has played an important role in the figures reported for 1956/7. Fuel rationing imposed during that time led to a curtailment of services, fewer miles run, and therefore to a reduced fare income. A fuel surcharge of 1s per gallon during the crisis added to these costs. As a result of these factors, the net revenue shows a deficit of £124,052 and an overall deficiency of £20,463 is reported. Of greater longer-term concern is a continuing drop in passenger numbers, which is attributed to 'the changing habits of the population caused by the increasing popularity of

Left: One of the two spray painting booths installed at Tyburn Road Works and inaugurated in October 1958. Used for spraying hot varnish, the booths both speeded up the process and saved £4 per bus treated. In this view a movable platform has been raised around Daimler CVD6 No 1974 of 1949. *Passenger Transport/IAL*

Above: In December 1958 the 15B service was extended to Meadway at Lea Hall and renumbered 17. Here No 1927, a Daimler CVG6 of 1948/9, is seen on the new service in Garretts Green Lane. *Robert B. McCann/IAL*

television and…the large number of motor-assisted cycles and other vehicles with low petrol consumption which have become very popular'. The mention of 'other vehicles with low petrol consumption' was an oblique reference to bubblecars, whose popularity was growing at this time.

April — The Council is reminded that the city centre layout is much as it had been at the start of the 19th century, save for the construction of Corporation Street and its associated roads, yet the volume of traffic is growing alarmingly. In places, traffic intensity has increased between 25% and 42% from 1950 to 1954.

2 July — In its annual report the Transport Committee notes a staff shortage of 638, of which the most significant are 286 drivers and 276 conductors. Much of this shortfall is being made up by existing staff working overtime.

21 July — A new bus service is introduced between Navigation Street and the Wychall Farm Estate, Kings Norton, and services to Weoley Castle are reorganised with the introduction of a new service 21 between Suffolk Street and Moors Lane, the renumbering of the present 20B as service 22, and the withdrawal of the 20, 20A, 20D and 20E.

28 July — A new fare structure is introduced.

1 September — The Department takes over the first stage of the former 'Midland Red' City-New Oscott service, by running the City-Beeches Estate, Perry Barr service. This had been operated on behalf of the Council since the boundary extensions of 1928. The city terminus was in Martineau Street.

7 December — The 15B service is extended to Garretts Green Lane/Meadway junction.

1958: A QUICK FINISH

Once again the Transport Department's fleet remained almost static: during the year no new vehicles were acquired, and just one, a Daimler COG5 from 1937, was withdrawn.

31 March — The Transport Department's fleet comprises 1,823 buses. Its end of year figures for 1957/8 show a net revenue surplus of £87,591 and an overall surplus of £106,795. A useful income for the Department comes from the 'Free Travel Scheme for Aged Persons', which brings in £90,000 from the General Purposes Committee, yet costs just £665 to administer. The letting of advertising on buses raises in an additional £92,911.

4 May — The Department takes over the second stage of the former 'Midland Red' City-New Oscott service by running the City-Great Barr via Walsall Road service.

31 July — The Transport Department's Chief Accountant, Mr P. Harold Wigley, retires, having been an employee of the Corporation since 23 July 1917.

September — The Department takes over the third and final stage of the former Midland Red City-New Oscott service by running the City-New Oscott via College Road service.

October — The Transport Department unveils two new spray paint booths at Tyburn Road Works for spray finishing with varnish. Tests with this process began in 1952, and evaluation of the vehicles has shown that the finish is standing up well. By 1956 the Department had been facing both a shortage of brush painters and an increase in the number of buses. This indicated that 15 would need to pass through the paint shop each week, whereas it had a capacity of just 11. The new spray booths, in addition to speeding up the process, offer a net saving of £4 per bus, or £3,000 over a year.

1959: A LIMITED FAILURE

The Public Works Committee approved a scheme to relight the principal traffic routes serving the city this year, with improved electric street lights. Eventually 155 miles of routes would be covered in this way, the scheme not being completed until 1968, at a total cost of £780,000. Meanwhile, the Transport Department's concern over the number of private motor vehicles being licensed each year was due to deepen following the unveiling of a certain new car at Longbridge that August.

16 February — A service of Limited Stop buses is introduced on an experimental basis between James Watt Street and the Tile Cross Estate as a modification to the 14 service. These leave the city at 5-6min intervals from

Above: Tram tracks are still in situ 20 years after they were needed at Hockley garage in 1959. Daimler CVD6 No 2747 of 1951 and Guy Arab II 5LW of 1945 both had over 10 years' more service left with the Corporation, being withdrawn in 1971 and 1968 respectively. *Robert F. Mack/D. R. Harvey Collection*

Above right: This view of the junction of Hill/Navigation/John Bright street was taken from a window in the Technical College in 1959. The crane in the background is working on the first phase of the Inner Ring Road, and work to rebuild New Street station would start in four years' time.
R. S. Carpenter Photos/Author's collection

Right: In the month that the Mini was launched at Longbridge, just under a half of Birmingham Corporation's bus fleet was 10 or more years old. Seen in Colmore Row in August 1959, working the 15 service to Yardley, is No 2141, a Leyland PD2/1 of 1949, which remained in service until 1967. *G. H. F. Atkins*

4.45pm to 6.30pm, and Tile Cross between 5.16pm and 6.05pm. At best a 6min reduction in running time can be achieved over the regular 14 service, and passenger loadings are light. For example, in the peak between 5.45pm and 6.14pm, on six buses travelling from the city, there are just 62 people. Loadings into the city are much lighter and after a three-month trial the service is withdrawn on 20 May.

31 March — The Transport Department's fleet comprises 1,823 buses. Its annual report shows an increased net revenue surplus of £292,927 and a net overall surplus of £434,924, but concern is still expressed at the overall decline in passenger numbers 'due to the still rapidly increasing number of motor scooters and other private motor vehicles which are being licensed annually'.

August — The launch of the Austin Super Seven, or Mini — the car which brought about a revolution in popular motoring. It was designed at Longbridge by Alec Issigonis, and is built by workers, most of whom travel there by Birmingham Corporation buses.

30 November — Staff shortages continue to cause problems. On this day there is a shortfall of 384 drivers and 542 conductors, and on occasions over 100 or so buses cannot be crewed.

4. 1960-69: 'One-Man' to the End

By 1960 Birmingham was being choked by traffic, and although the first stage of the Inner Ring Road opened that year, it would be a long time before the scheme was completed and the full benefit of the relief it offered felt. For the Transport Department, its construction was just one more hazard to be dealt with. Its principal concerns were:
• falling passenger numbers;
• increasing employment costs; and,
• staff shortages which now topped 1,000.

It was not alone in this, and the bus manufacturers responded by offering transport operators larger capacity double-deckers, seating 72 to 77 people, the thinking being that if the available passengers could be carried on fewer buses, then operating costs could be reduced whilst fare revenue remained the same. Birmingham Corporation was certainly interested and took delivery of demonstration models made by AEC, Daimler, Guy and Leyland for trial purposes. These proved successful and the choice was narrowed to two: the Daimler Fleetline and Leyland Atlantean. To enable a final choice to be made, 10 of each model were ordered for an extensive trial which eventually came out in favour of the Fleetline, also reflecting a loyalty to the manufacturer which had supplied so much of the former bus fleets, with its prewar COG5s and postwar CVD and CVG6s.

Elsewhere the city tackled its traffic problems by building off-road car parks and by beginning a massive road improvement programme which would see out the decade to complete. By the time that the first order of 100 Daimler Fleetline buses was delivered in 1963, the city also had its first parking meters and their companions: traffic wardens.

Another means of reducing operating costs was to have the drivers do the job of the conductor, and collect fares. One-Man Operation, or 'OMO', had obvious savings, but clear limitations too, especially on heavily loaded services where long stays at stops to collect fares would not add to the efficiency of the service. Accordingly, when Birmingham Corporation introduced OMO services in

1963, it was on a new lightly loaded 'feeder' service and involved single-deck buses. As with everything the Transport Department did, this service was experimental at first and closely monitored. Pronounced a success in 1964, OMO was introduced on more new services, until, in 1966, an existing service was changed over to this form of operation. Inevitably, OMO double-deckers followed, first on Sunday services, but then throughout the week, and new buses were delivered ready equipped for the purpose.

Now in direct competition with the private car, the Transport Department also had another try at providing a Limited Stop service, and experimented with both formal and ad hoc Park-&-Ride schemes. By 1968 these seemed to be the directions in which the bus service was headed, but that year saw the coming into law of a revised Transport Act, paving the way for the establishment of four Passenger Transport Executives, one of which was to be in the West Midlands. Accordingly, after 65 years, Birmingham Corporation ceased to be a transport operator on 1 October 1969.

1960: MORE ROOM ON TOP

As the first stage of the Inner Ring Road was completed, the benefits of the whole scheme could be gauged, even if they were a long way off. The Transport Department's main concerns remained staff shortages and employment costs, with the latter set to rise yet again following a compulsory reduction in working hours. Demonstration models of four types of bus offering larger seating capacities were obtained for comparative trials, these being one each of the AEC Bridgemaster, Guy Wulfrunian, Leyland Atlantean and Daimler Fleetline. No other new vehicles were acquired this year, and 41 older buses were withdrawn: one Daimler COG5 from 1936; 39 Daimler COG5s from 1937 and one Daimler COG5 from 1939.

January — A joint report by the Public Works and Watch committees notes that whilst traffic maintains an average of 12mph off-peak, and 10mph peak, through the city, the main causes of delays are vehicles parked on the radial roads. In response, the Council issues a series of No Waiting orders restricting vehicle loading, particularly in the 4.30pm-6.30pm evening peak.

11 March — Ernest Marples, the Minister of Transport, opens the first section of the Inner Ring Road.

28 March — A compulsory reduction in working hours is introduced, making bus crewing problems all the harder for the Transport Department.

31 March — The Transport Department's fleet remains at 1,823 buses. In the annual report for 1959/60 there is a

Left: In 1960 Birmingham Corporation conducted comparative trials using demonstration models of four types of bus offering larger seating capacities: AEC Bridgemaster, Guy Wulfrunian, Leyland Atlantean and Daimler Fleetline. This is the Daimler, which acquired the city coat of arms, but retained the company name where the General Manager's was usually applied. *Passenger Transport/IAL*

net revenue surplus of £298,038 and an increased overall surplus of £646,397. An additional concern comes from a change in the terms of the Department's insurance under which its insurers will only pay out on claims under catastrophic risk cover above £10,000; for claims below this level the Department will have to pay out directly. As a contingency for this, £200,000 is set aside in the General Reserve Fund.

1 April — A car park is opened to the southwest of Dudley Street, under the Inner Ring Road, but initially it is very unpopular with motorists.

31 May — The staff shortage worsens. The Transport Department now requires 535 drivers and 551 conductors, and on some days as many as 166 buses have no crew. Much of the service still relies on overtime working.

5 June — A compulsory 42hr working week is introduced for manual staff.

5 July — In an attempt to head off falling passenger numbers the Transport Department takes to advertising on its own buses. The upper rear panels of double-deck vehicles carry the slogan: '*AVOID THE RACE FOR A CAR PARK SPACE — TAKE A BUS TO ANY PLACE.*'

29 September — The opening of an extension to the Museum of Science & Industry into which preserved Birmingham tramcar No 395 has been moved. Prior to this opening, painters from the Transport Department repaint the car — the last time its employees work on a Birmingham tram.

November — The Minister of Transport approves a scheme, first submitted by the city's Public Works Committee in 1958, for a 12-15 year rolling programme of road improvements in Birmingham, divided into small (less that £100,000) and large (more than £100,000) schemes. The six largest schemes are:

• Parts of the Inner Ring Road
• Rubery Bypass
• Six Ways Aston Underpass
• Nechells Green Parkway
• Hockley Hill Flyover
• Aston Road-Lichfield Road (Aston Expressway)

In total the road improvements are estimated to cost £30 million.

10 December — The staff shortage problem has eased slightly, but the Department is still short of 379 drivers and 270 conductors and the service is being maintained by overtime and rest day working.

1961: A CHOICE OF TWO

Comparative trials with larger capacity double-deckers favoured the Daimler Fleetline and Leyland Atlantean, and 10 of each were ordered to allow for more extensive testing before a large order was placed. Now also acting as its own vehicle tester, the Transport Department found some of its buses too unsound to remain in service. Eleven new buses were delivered, including 10 Leyland Atlanteans with 72-seat bodies by Metropolitan-Cammell (Nos 3231-40).

Above: From 15 February 1961 the Transport Department acted as its own vehicle tester and found some of its buses too unsound to remain in service. Much of the fleet, like Daimler CVG6 No 1600 of 1947, was over 10 years old. It is seen entering Hill Street from Navigation Street. *R. H. G. Simpson*

10 January — The Transport Committee reports that regulations now permit longer and wider buses, up to 30ft by 8ft, and that a double-deck vehicle of these dimensions could seat up to 78 persons. Tests with hired, borrowed or single-purchased vehicles have led the Department to conclude that the ideal formulation for such a bus is one with a seating capacity of not less that 72, heating and ventilation in the upper and lower saloons, with a front entrance, fitted with automatic doors, in advance of the front wheels. This specification suits two production chassis, and more extensive tests are indicated. Accordingly, the purchase of 10 Leyland Atlantean and 10 Daimler Fleetline chassis is recommended, with bodies on each built by Metropolitan-Cammell of Birmingham.

15 February — The compulsory testing of vehicles under the terms of the Road Traffic Act, 1956, is introduced. In preparation for this a Vehicle Testing Station has been created at Miller Street garage, where buses have been tested voluntarily since 12 September 1960. Between then and 30 May 1961, 1,521 buses are tested, of which 907 pass and 614 fail, and 405 are subsequently retested. The testing facilities are also available to outside users.

31 March — After years remaining static, the Transport Department's fleet has declined and comprises 1,781 buses. In the accounts for 1960/1, whilst revenue shows a surplus of £665,588, this is more than absorbed by loan repayments and other charges, including those arising from an enlargement of Tyburn Road Works, giving an overall revenue deficit of £57,059. Overall the Department declares a surplus of £615,408, but caution is expressed over increased employment costs, mainly from pay awards, which have cost an additional £631,000 in the last year alone.

May — The Leyland Atlantean demonstration vehicle acquired in 1960 is purchased and becomes No 3230 in the fleet.

4 July — The Transport Committee reports that owing to a progressive falling off in passenger numbers, the 57B bus service between Yardley and Station Street is to be withdrawn. This will produce a saving of £7,500 a year.

19 November — A new fare schedule is introduced.

1962: A Change at the Top

Nine years after the end of tramway operation in Birmingham, the main link to those times was through the Transport Department staff whose service included tram work. None more so than with the General Manager, who presided over the final tramway abandonment, Mr W. H. Smith. He retired this year, and was succeeded by his deputy, who became the last ever General Manager of the undertaking.

9 January — The Transport Committee reports that the 20 new buses ordered in January 1961 have now been delivered, the last being 10 Daimler CRG6 Fleetlines with 77-seat bodies by Metropolitan-Cammell (Nos 3241-50). All 20 vehicles are now being tried on the 43 (City-Nechells) and 96 (City-Lodge Road-Winson Green) to evaluate them under intensive conditions.

31 March — The Transport Department's fleet continues to decline, particularly in the face of the compulsory vehicle testing, and now comprises 1,719 buses. In the 1961/2 financial year a revenue surplus of £276,456 produced, but when the necessary charges have been paid

Above: In 1962 Birmingham Corporation undertook an extensive evaluation of 10 77-seat Daimler CRG6 Fleetlines and 10 76-seat Leyland Atlanteans on the 43 (City-Nechells) and 96 (City-Lodge Road-Winson Green) services. Here No 3232, the second of the 10 Atlanteans, is seen in the heart of the city's Jewellery Quarter. *Ron Moss*

from this, a deficit of £419,070 is created to be carried forward, and the overall surplus is just £177,276.

14 July — Highgate Road garage closes. It had been built as a tramcar depot in 1913 and opened as an omnibus garage in June 1937.

8 August — The General Manager of the Transport Department, Mr W. H. Smith, reaches the age of 65 today and retires. He is succeeded by his deputy, Mr W. G. Copestake, who relinquishes his post as Chief Engineer, being succeeded there by his deputy, Mr H. R. Robinson, who has worked for the Department since 1936.

9 September — The annual fare revision takes effect today.

Left: Ten years separate No 1616 Daimler CVG6 of 1947 and BMMO D7 No 4548 of 1957 as they approach Old Square along Corporation Street in 1962. The Daimler had just one more year in Corporation service to go. *R. H. G. Simpson*

Below left: Crossley No 1648 was one of 10 delivered in 1949, whilst brand-new BMMO S15 No 5045 was the first in a batch of 48 which entered service in the year of this photograph — 1962. The X99 service worked between the city and Nottingham via Ashby-de-la-Zouch. *R. H. G. Simpson*

Above: No 3231, the first of the batch of 10 new Leyland Atlanteans delivered in 1961, is seen loading in Corporation Street in 1962. These vehicles were part of an extended comparison with Daimler's Fleetline chassis conducted that year. *T. W. Moore*

Below: Under trial Atlantean No 3233 was photographed by the College of Arts & Crafts in Margaret Street, working the 96 service in August 1962. Midland Red D5 No 3476 still looks quite modern in comparison, despite being built in 1949/50. *T. W. Moore*

1963: One Man Went to …

By its first Parking Meter Order the City Council created 856 parking meter bays in an attempt to restrict parking to designated places and cut down the disruption caused to traffic by indiscriminate parking. The profit from the meters was supposed to be ploughed into off-street parking, but in the first four years of operation in Birmingham this barely paid for the capital outlay, and a 40% allocation to Traffic Warden wages contributed to a £30,788 overall loss on the scheme by 1967. Bus services were supposed to benefit from this move. A hundred new Daimler CRG6 Fleetlines were ordered and entered service later in the year, 50 having bodies by Park Royal (Nos 3251-300) and 50 with bodies by Metropolitan-Cammell (Nos 3301-3350). In December the

Left: Daimler Fleetline No 3252 was one of 50 having bodies by Park Royal (Nos 3251-3300). It is pictured here as it enters service on 7 July 1963 on the 39. *IAL*

Below: Prior to delivery to Birmingham, body makers Park Royal had No 3255 photographed. Seen here is a rear three-quarter view showing the bus's clean lines. The Fleetlines offered passengers levels of light and room they were unaccustomed to. *Park Royal Vehicles Ltd/IAL*

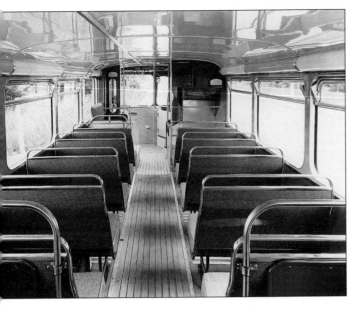

This page: Detailed views of Park Royal-bodied Fleetline No 3262 were also recorded before it entered service. Shown here is the lower saloon; shots of the upper saloon; a close-up of the front entrance, with the driver's slanted windscreen; and the front platform and driver's cab.
Park Royal Vehicles Ltd/IAL

provision of a new service to a housing estate provided an opportunity to evaluate 'OMO' bus operation.

5 February — With the tests of the new larger buses complete, the Transport Department feels able to commit itself to placing a large order. The Committee reports that 'these larger type omnibuses have been very well received by the travelling public and the operating staff and many expressions of appreciation of the improved facilities provided in the new vehicles have been received. [Their] performance has been most satisfactory so far as economy is concerned.' As a result, the Department has ordered 300 Daimler Fleetline chassis from Transport Vehicles (Daimler) Ltd, with 150 bodies each to be supplied by Park Royal Vehicles Ltd of London and Metropolitan-Cammell of Birmingham. They will be delivered over the next 3 years. The Transport Committee also proposes 'to replace approximately one-fifteenth of the fleet each year and to meet the replacement costs out of revenue. This will avoid the borrowing of money…(and) will also enable a balanced programme of maintenance work to be operated.'

31 March — The Transport Department's fleet is still declining, and is now 1,717 buses. In the accounts for 1962/3 a net revenue surplus of £347,428 is declared, and an overall surplus of £620,438.

23 July — After being requested to do so by the Council in November 1962, the Transport Committee has reconsidered its ban on Sikhs wearing turbans whilst engaged as drivers or conductors, and reversed its decision. Navy blue uniform turbans must be worn.

October — With Birmingham the central focus of the growing West Midlands conurbation, the Ministry of Transport has approached the City Council with a view to

Above: One of 50 buses delivered in 1963, Daimler Fleetline No 3316 had a 72-seat MCW body. It is seen parked on the Coventry Road on 20 May 1967. The vehicle remained in service with WMPTE until 1977. *G. Mead/IAL*

Above right: According to its service indicators, new Daimler Fleetline No 3262 is going either to Wharf Road, on Pershore Road South (45F), or to Six Ways, Aston. In fact, it's another maker's shot showing the styling of the 76-seat Park Royal bodies. *Park Royal Vehicles Ltd/IAL*

Right: This view across St Martin's Circus on 31 July 1964 was taken from the Bull Ring multi-storey car park, and once adorned the cover of the 1965 Ian Allan *abc of Birmingham Buses*. In the foreground, new Fleetline No 3358 is followed by Guy No 2596 of 1950/1, whilst behind Wimpey's workers complete the Rotunda. *T. W. Moore/IAL*

conducting a comprehensive survey of transport facilities with a view to their long-term strategic planning. This is receiving consideration.

1 December — In response to representations made over a number of years, the Transport Committee institutes a bus service to serve tenants on the Pool Farm Estate in Fox Hollies. This is achieved by running a feeder service of buses down Walkers Heath and Hillmeads roads from Cotteridge, and follows the provision of a suitable turning circle at the junction of Hillmeads and Sisefield roads by the Public Works Committee. The service is provided by single-deck OMO vehicles, and it will also serve as an experiment in the working of these vehicles.

Left: As a break from the flat-fronted styling of earlier Daimler Fleetlines, the MCW-bodied batch (Nos 3351-450) delivered in 1964 featured a relief-moulded front which aped a radiator. On 4 January 1965 No 3393 is seen in Corporation Street, returning to the city from Witton. *T. W. Moore/IAL*

Above: In July 1964, as the first of many generations of 'TO LET' signs are pasted to the windows of the Rotunda, work is well advanced on the rebuilding of Birmingham New Street station (on the left) as Leyland PD2 No 2191 works past on the soon to be renumbered 29A service. *T. W. Moore*

Below: All of those responsible for the Rotunda — the symbol of the new city, are proudly displayed behind Crossley No 2417 as it passes the corner of High Street in July 1964 on the 44 service. *T. W. Moore*

1964: A NATURAL FOCUS

Birmingham's place as the natural focus of the West Midlands conurbation was becoming recognised, and the City Council decided to act upon an approach from the Ministry of Transport last October and conducted a comprehensive transport facilities survey with a view to their strategic planning long-term. The OMO experiment in Fox Hollies had proved successful, and the Transport Department looked to other services on which the method of working could be tried. They also ordered a further 100 Daimler CRG6 Fleetlines.

26 January — A new fare structure is introduced.

31 March — The Transport Department's fleet has declined further and now stands at 1,681 buses. Figures for the financial year 1963/4 show a net revenue deficiency of £261,736 to be carried forward, and an overall surplus of £325,262.

4 February — A contribution of £60,000 is pledged by the City Council towards the estimated £250,000 cost of the comprehensive transport survey proposed last October. On 31 August 1964 a conurbation-wide steering committee established to oversee the survey work appoint Messrs Freeman, Fox, Wilbur Smith & Associates to carry out the work.

July — 48 Daimler CRG6 Fleetlines, with 76-seat bodies by Metropolitan-Cammell, are delivered (Nos 3351-98).

Above: Daimler Fleetline No 3270 was about as new as much of the roadway it ran on when it emerged from the Bull Ring in July 1964 on to St Martin's Circus Ringway. It was also unsure as to whether it was working the 60 service from Cranes Park or the 58 from Sheldon. *T. W. Moore*

Above right: St Martin's Church in the Bull Ring provides a dark backdrop to Crossley No 2331 of 1950 on a July day in 1964 as the skies begin to darken. The bus had just two more years service with Birmingham Corporation. *T. W. Moore*

Right: Immediate postwar buses, such as Daimler CVG6 No 1866 of 1948/9, were still the mainstay of the fleet the Fleetlines entered. On the Inner Circle service 8, No 1866 is seen in Icknield Street in May 1964. *Ron Moss*

21 July — Reporting back on the evaluation of the use of single-deck OMO buses to serve the Pool Farm Estate in Fox Hollies, the Transport Committee deems this a great success. Where the number of passengers to be carried is relatively small, the use of such vehicles is recommended, and their employment elsewhere is under consideration. The next route these buses are likely to be introduced on is another feeder service, running from the Vicarage/Alcester road junction in Kings Heath, along Allen's Croft and Brandwood Park roads.

WITTON
VIA ASTON CROSS

39

FROM CITY

393 KOV

Ten of the 48 Daimler CRG6 Fleetlines (Nos 3351-3398) delivered from July 1964 had experimental windscreens, with much reduced centre pillars. Four of the 10 also had curved windscreens, but No 3393, seen here in Corporation Street on 3 January 1965, had flat screens mounted in a 'V' pattern. *T. W. Moore/IAL*

1965: OLD BUSES RETURN

Whilst making moves to reduce the overall number of staff it required, the Transport Department was once again in the midst of an acute staff shortage, requiring 800 drivers and conductors. It also entered into an historic agreement with a private bus operator to serve housing around Aldridge, outside the city's boundaries. Rather than just working to the boundary, the operator, Harper Brothers Ltd was allowed to work through to the city centre. Being an operator of ex-Corporation vehicles, this meant that some might return to their former streets. The year also saw 100 more Daimler CRG6 Fleetlines ordered. Vehicles entering service included: 24 OMO 37-seat single-deck Daimler CRG6s, with bodies by Marshall (Nos 3451-74); 14 Daimler CRG6 Fleetlines, with 76-seat bodies by Metropolitan-Cammell (Nos 3399-400; 3525-6) and 40 Daimler CRG6 Fleetlines, with 76-seat bodies by Park Royal (Nos 3475-514). A further five large capacity single-deck buses, one each of Bedford VAM, AEC Swift, Bristol RELL6G, Leyland PSUR1/1 and Daimler SRC6, were obtained for trials.

2 February — After improving over recent years, staff shortages are once again acute, with over 800 vacancies for drivers and conductors. These are causing late and irregular running of services, particularly in the peak periods, and are contributing to the continuing decline in passengers.

8 February — Analysis of the cost of providing All-Night buses, and the use made of them, shows that they have a relatively small number of passengers, especially between 1am and 4.30am. As a result, from this date the former flat 1s 3d fare for these buses is replaced by a two-tier system, with 2s being charged during this slack period, and 1s 6d being charged at other times.

31 March — The Transport Department's fleet has increased slightly and is now 1,683 buses. The figures for 1965/6 show an increased net revenue surplus of £764,838 and an overall surplus of £439,734.

21 June — The growth of large housing developments around Aldridge has led to requests for a bus service between there and the city, but it lies outside the city, and therefore outside the area in which Corporation services can operate. To provide this link a private operator, Harper Brothers Ltd, of Heath Hayes, had run double-deck buses through Aldridge from Cannock to Kingstanding, where passengers could connect with Corporation buses. Under the terms of an agreement which comes into effect on this date, Harper Brothers gain a licence to run through from Kingstanding to Union

Street in the city centre. The same powers are also granted to Walsall Corporation, which had also been working through to Kingstanding. Ironically, Harper Brothers have been great purchasers and operators of former Birmingham Corporation vehicles.

3 October — A new schedule of fares is introduced.

1966: FIVE DAYS A WEEK

Two further changes in employment law — a five-day week for platform staff, and a 40hr week for unskilled workers — were expected to improve staff recruitment, but also raise employment costs. There were additional concerns when the annual rate of decline in passenger numbers doubled. A City Sightseeing Tour was run in the summer to coincide with the World Cup, and three new OMO feeder services were introduced later in the year to further the evaluation of this form of operation. The year's bus orders included 76 (reduced from 100) Daimler CRG6 Fleetlines, with 76-seat bodies by Metropolitan-Cammell (Nos 3537-612) and 23 Daimler CRG6 Fleetlines, with 76-seat bodies by Park Royal (Nos 3515-24; 3613-25).

Above: In March 1965 Birmingham Corporation took delivery of 24 OMO 37-seat single-deck Daimler CRG6 Fleetlines (Nos 3451-3474), with bodies by Marshall. The first in the batch is seen heading down Pershore Road South working on the Cotteridge-Pool Farm Estate service 4, the first OMO route in the city. *T. W. Moore/IAL*

Above right: As the deliveries of new Fleetlines mounted up, the older vehicles in the Corporation's fleet were withdrawn. The future catches up with Daimler CVG6 No 1910 of 1948/9 one night in Bull Street. *T. W. Moore/IAL*

Right: Ordered in 1965, Daimler Fleetline No 3552 was delivered in January 1966, and is seen passing Lyons Cornerhouse and the Fleur de Lys night club as it rounds Victoria Square into New Street. The following year the vehicle was equipped for One-Man Operation. *T. W. Moore*

2 January — A five-day week is introduced for all platform staff on the Transport Department's buses. An anticipated improvement in staff recruitment following on from this does not materialise.

3 January — A compulsory 40hr working week is intro-

Left: Seen on 27 June 1966, the year of its withdrawal, No 2326, a Crossley of 1949/50, climbs Hill Street on the 32 service, whilst being cut up by an Aston-Martin. *T. W. Moore/IAL*

Above: A notice for the sightseeing tours of the city at its loading point in Colmore Row. The trilingual wording was because of the World Cup, some of the matches of which were played at Villa Park, but little is given away as to what sights people were taken to see! *R. Ashton/IAL*

Above right: It wasn't just foreign visitors who were taken on trips around Birmingham by bus in 1966; one Corporation vehicle, Fleetline No 3575, went on tour to Lyon in France, Birmingham's twin city. *Modern Transport/IAL*

duced for unskilled workers. The Transport Department estimates that this will cost an additional £350,000 per year.

1 February — In accordance with its policy of replacing one-15th of its bus fleet each year, the Transport Committee has ordered 276 Daimler Fleetline chassis, with 138 bodies each being made by Park Royal Vehicles Ltd, London, and Metropolitan-Cammell of Birmingham. An order of 24 OMO buses has been delivered and these have been placed in service on suitable routes.

27 February — An OMO single-deck bus service 57 is introduced between the Castle Vale Estate and the Fox & Goose at Washwood Heath.

31 March — The Transport Department's fleet has increased and is now 1,697 buses. In the Transport

Committee's report for 1965/6 it is noted that an operating revenue surplus £618,934 has been used to reduce other deficits and make payments, producing an overall revenue deficit of £116,568. The overall surplus is £441,718.

11 July — Sightseeing tours of the city by bus are inaugurated, running from Colmore Row, to coincide with the World Cup, some of the matches of which are being played at Villa Park. There are two trips a day, each lasting for 1¼hr at a cost of 2s 6d for adults and 1s 3d for children. The tours run daily until 24 July, and, rather ambitiously, the notice for them is in English, Spanish and German.

19 July — The Transport Committee reports that the decline in passengers, which had been at around 3% per year, has accelerated to 6% during 1965/6. Unfortunately, there is no discernible pattern to this decline, which gives rise to great concern. Following the successful introduction of OMO buses on new feeder services to the Pool Farm (4), Brandwood Park (35) and Castle Vale (57) estates, the Kings Heath-West Heath service 27 has been converted to their operation. This is the first time such a conversion has been made in the city, and it has worked well. Now it is proposed to convert the Stechford-Stoney Lane service (36), for which 18 new buses have been ordered. Other services are also being studied with a view to similar conversions taking place.

August — The former Birchfield Road tram depot, latterly a bus garage, closes as an operational garage with the withdrawal of the last Daimler CVA6 buses. It is retained for the storage of withdrawn buses.

Left: By the time that Fleetline No 3587 was delivered in 1966 there had been many detail changes to the body, including the windscreen, grilles for the improved heating, and better interior lighting. It was one of a reduced order of 76 Daimler CRG6s, with 76-seater bodies by Metropolitan-Cammell (Nos 3537-612). *IAL*

Below left: Driverless Fleetline No 3618 is in danger of losing two women passengers from outside the Odeon in New Street, but perhaps they are not queuing correctly. Meanwhile, Daimler CVG6 No 3164 tries to pull out from behind, working the 90 service. *T. W. Moore/IAL*

Above: Looking like someone out of a DAKS advert, a sharp-suited young man is oblivious to the fate of Crossley No 2291, which is being towed up the Bull Ring by service vehicle 51, formerly a Corporation Daimler COG5 omnibus. No 2291 was withdrawn in 1966. *T. W. Moore*

Below: Winkles are a-picking and hemlines a-rising in New Street on 16 May 1966. Fleetline 3542, delivered in April 1965, celebrates its first year in Corporation service with a run on the 24 service to Warstock, one of the few routes left unaltered since it was introduced in November 1930. *T. W. Moore*

Locally made cars are prominent in this view of the top end of New Street in July 1966. Crossley No 2338 was part of a massive order of 130 delivered in 1949/50, and was working its last year in service before withdrawal in 1967. *T. W. Moore*

1967: WHY NOT PARK-&-RIDE?

Great advances were made in the development of OMO bus services this year. To date, all of the OMO services had only worked outside the city centre, but from mid-January one ran through to Colmore Circus. Also, one of the experimental OMO feeder services proved so successful that it was also worked by double-deck buses. Following on from trials of five types of large capacity single-deckers, the Ford R192 46-seater was chosen, and 12 of them, with bodies by Strachan (3651-3662), entered service this year; the first equipped for OMO from new. As a trial of more extensive working of OMO double-deckers, they worked three services on Sundays. In other service innovations, a Park-&-Ride Limited Stop service was introduced into the city along the Bristol Road, and, later in the year, regular services worked by OMO double-deckers were introduced, a first in the country. The West Midlands

Conurbation transport study also reported this year and found in favour of a Rapid Transit system, plus bus lanes and junction priority systems. Yet another 100 Daimler CRG6LX Fleetlines were ordered in 1967, and bus deliveries included 25 Daimler CRG6 Fleetlines, with 76-seat bodies by Park Royal (Nos 3626-50). Five of these (Nos 3608-12) were converted for one-man operation in 1967, and four more (3613-16) in 1968. Also delivered were 18 AEC Swift chassis, with Metropolitan-Cammell single-deck bodies, having separate entrance and exit doors for OMO (3663-80). Each had seats for 37, with the first 12 being 33ft long and having standing room for 30, and the last six being 36ft long and having standing room for 39. Finally, 50 of the Daimler CRG6LX Fleetlines ordered earlier in the year were delivered, with 76-seater bodies by Metropolitan-Cammell (Nos 3681-730).

15 January — A new bus service 46 is introduced from Queslett-Colmore Circus via Aldridge Road. This is the first OMO service to work into the city centre.

3 February — Messrs Freeman, Fox, Wilbur Smith & Associates, appointed on 31 August 1964 to carry out a comprehensive transport survey of the West Midlands conurbation, produce their technical report. This suggests

Above: Flags still fly on the shopping centre as two girls become a blur dashing for Fleetline No 3384, working the 50 service to the Maypole, at the top of the Bull Ring on a rainy evening in January 1967. *T. W. Moore*

Left: After trials of five types of large capacity single-deckers, the Ford R192 46-seater was chosen and 12 were ordered, with bodies by Strachans (Nos 3651-62), the first two being OMO-equipped from new. No 3651, the first in the batch, is seen on driver training duty outside Selly Oak garage. *IAL*

road and junction improvements, and improved bus services utilising reserved lanes and junction priority systems. A Lifford-Selly Oak-Five Ways-Winson Green-Perry Barr-Aston-Moseley 'figure-of-eight' rail service is also proposed, as is a rapid transit system between Wolverhampton and Olton.

7 February — The Transport Committee reports that the 57 service, from the Castle Vale Estate to the Fox & Goose at Washwood Heath, has proven so successful that it has been extended deeper into the estate, and at times has had to be operated by double-deck buses. Now it is proposed to link the estate to Erdington and the city centre by modifying the route of the 66 service through Castle Vale. It is also reported that sufficient numbers of large capacity Daimler 'Fleetline' double-deck buses have been delivered to enable the entire operation of 15 services to be given wholly over to them.

Above: With its conductor's head in a flare of light, Daimler Fleetline No 3604 waits to enter Corporation Street from Union Street on service 42. In preparation for the introduction of OMO double-deckers, on Sundays from 11 June 1967, this was one of three services worked by such buses especially fitted with power-operated ticket machines and periscopes so the driver could see the seats upstairs. *T. W. Moore/IAL*

Right: On 16 July 1967 the Lodge Road route (96) became solely operated by OMO double-deckers; the first such conversion in any city in the country. No 3547, an OMO-converted 76 seat Daimler Fleetline CRG6 of 1965, is seen passing the premises of Thomas Fattorini Ltd in Frederick Street, working the route. *Ron Moss*

The services concerned are Nos 1 (Acocks Green-Moseley), 3 (Ridgacre Lane via Harborne), 12 (Bartley Green via Harborne), 13 (Ravenshill Road-School Road-Yardley Wood), 14 (Tile Cross Estate via Kitts Green), 24 (Warstock via Showell Green Lane), 33 (Kingstanding via Six Ways, Aston), 38 (Yardley Wood via Stoney Lane), 39 (Witton via Aston Cross), 43 (Nechells), 50 (Maypole via Bradford Street), 55 (Shard End Estate), 58 (Sheldon via Coventry Road), 60 (Cranes Park Estate via Coventry Road) and 96 (Winson Green via Lodge Road). In addition, all of the All-Night services are operated by these vehicles. OMO single-deck buses are also now operating successfully on five services, including the 46 (Aldridge Road-Colmore Circus). In order to introduce this kind of service on other services, 24 existing 34-seater single-deckers are to be converted to OMO, and 12 new 46-seater single-deckers are to be ordered with which to try an experimental Limited Stop service with OMO vehicles along the Bristol Road.

21 February — The vacant post of Deputy General Manager has been filled by Mr C. Nurse, a Superintendent in the Traffic Department.

31 March — The Transport Department's fleet has decreased again and is now 1,601 buses. In the financial year 1966/7 revenue surplus is £298,364, which becomes a deficit of £419,074 when other charges have been made from it, to be carried forward. Overall, a net surplus of £315,337 is declared. Outside use of the Vehicle Testing Station at Miller Street has been minimal, and the staff levels have been reduced to a minimum. It has been making an annual loss of around £2,000 a year, so the Transport Committee has decided to close it with effect from this date.

April — Birchfield Road garage closes completely after the disposal of the withdrawn buses it stored.

1 April — The contribution paid by the Council's General Purposes Committee for the Aged Persons Free Travel Scheme is increased from £120,000 to £150,000.

2 April — A new provisional fare structure is introduced. There is also a new bus service (47) which runs from Groveley Lane-Navigation Street and is worked in conjunction with the 41 service. This has required the provision or alteration of 12 bus stops.

3 April — Pioneering Park-&-Ride schemes are intro-

Above: No 3664 was one of 12 AEC Swifts, with separate entrance and exit doors for OMO. The Metropolitan-Cammell bodies were 33ft long, seated 37, and had standing room for a further 30. Registered in August 1967, the bus is seen on 28 September that year. *AEC Ltd/IAL*

Right: At Colmore Circus on 9 December 1967 AEC Swift No 3665 works a Christmas Shoppers' Special circular service around the city centre. Despite being equipped for OMO, conductors were used, but the service was not well patronised, even when the adult fare was dropped to 3d. Swifts Nos 3671 and 3672 were also used on the service. *E. N. Pounder/IAL*

duced from car parks in Rubery and Northfield on Mondays to Fridays. The parking fee entitles the car occupants to travel by a Limited Stop OMO single-deck bus into the city centre free of charge. The service, 99, makes just 3 stops and works well enough, but people are reluctant to use the buses for fear of leaving their car unattended for long periods.

24 May — Off the back of the West Midlands Transport Study a Joint Conference of Local Authority Officers recommends a Local Authority Team be established to carry out a study to produce a Transportation Plan for 1981. This is to be called the West Midlands Transport Study Group. Their remit is to look at:

• the main highway network;
• the public transport systems, including their operating standards; and
• the parking policies required by the above.

11 June — In preparation for services on heavily used services, experiments begin with the Sunday working of OMO double-deckers on the Sandon Road-City Centre (6), New Oscott-Union Street (42) and Nechells-Corporation Street (43) services. The vehicles have been fitted with power-operated TIM ticket machines and periscopes to enable the driver

to see how many empty seats there are upstairs.

16 July — The Transport Committee organises sightseeing tours of the city's redevelopment areas using buses equipped with loudspeaker systems. Two services tour the southern and northern areas of the city, and run until 27 September, during which time 5,461 passengers are carried. It is hoped to repeat the service next year, beginning on 3 June 1968. On the same day, the Lodge Road service (96) becomes solely operated by OMO double-deckers, the first such conversion in any city in the country.

18 July — Delivery is expected within the next few weeks of the single-deck OMO buses with which to work the Stechford-Stoney Lane service 36. The service mileage operated by these vehicles has increased markedly over the last two years. In the year to 31 March 1966 they worked 283,000 miles, in the year to 31 March 1967 839,000 miles, and by 31 March 1968 they are expected to have worked 1,700,000 miles.

27 August — The practice of separate ticketing for services operating in West Bromwich ends.

11 September — A new Bromford Bridge-Alum Rock

link service (26) is introduced, worked by two OMO single-deckers.

3 October — The Transport Committee expresses concern over how it is best to pay for the 100 buses outstanding from its order for 276 placed in 1965, due for delivery in 1968/9. The fare increases applied for in February have been turned down, and the end of year out-turn on 31 March shows a rolling deficit of £419,074, with a forecast fall in receipts for 1968/9 of a further £500,000. To compound this, the price of the vehicles has risen from £6,800 each when the first had been ordered in 1962, to £7,835 each today, but the specification has been changed to give 80 seats and to include central exit doors to permit OMO. As it seems unlikely that these can be paid for out of the Transport Department's revenue, the Committee has asked that the expenditure of approximately £800,000 be approved, and that an application be made to the Minister of Transport for loan sanction for this amount.

8 October — An OMO central-exit single-decker, No 3672, is introduced on the Stechford-Sparkbrook service (36).

4 November — As Christmas approaches the Rubery Limited Stop service (99) is also run on Saturdays from this date. The frequency is one every 15min between 10am and 6pm, but over the eight days it operates receipts are a quarter less than on weekdays, so the experiment is considered not worth repeating.

6 November — A new bus service (68) is introduced between the city and The Radleys/Sheldon Heath Road junction.

12 November — More experiments begin with OMO double-deck buses when they are introduced on Sundays only on the Acocks Green via Moseley service (1) and Acocks Green-Lincoln Road North service (44).

December — AEC Swift single-deckers are used on a Shoppers' Special Christmas Service, which circles the city centre following a New Street-Corporation Street-Bull Street-Colmore Circus-Priory Ringway-Corporation Street-High Street-Bull Ring Centre-Holloway Circus-Hill Street-New Street service. Despite being equipped for OMO, conductors are used, but the service does not attract many passengers.

1968: THE FINAL ACT

The supremacy of buses as the major public transport carrier in the West Midlands conurbation was confirmed by the final report from the Transport Study, which also recommended the integration of road and rail systems. OMO bus services became more widespread in the city, and ad hoc Park-&-Ride services were used with great success to move crowds to and from an FA Cup tie and the City of Birmingham Show. But all further development of transport services was put on notice by the Transport Act, 1968,

which came into law in October, establishing four Passenger Transport Executives, one of which was to be in the West Midlands. New bus deliveries included: 50 Daimler CRG6LX Fleetlines, with 76-seat Park Royal bodies (Nos 3731-80), followed by 33 Daimler CRG6LX Fleetlines, with 72-seat Park Royal bodies (Nos 3781-813), which were equipped for OMO from new.

1 January — Messrs Freeman, Fox, Wilbur Smith & Associates produce their final report. This records that 97% of people using public transport travel on buses, and that they are badly affected by traffic congestion. The suggested solution is an integrated transportation system, with improved rail and road transport.

27 January — An ad hoc Park-&-Ride service is tried on the occasion of an FA Cup tie at Villa Park. A total of 16 journeys are made, carrying 770 people from Dunlop Car Park to Villa Park and back. Deemed a success, other opportunities are sought on which to repeat the experiment.

31 March — Reporting its annual figures for 1967/8, the Transport Committee shows an overall revenue deficit of £236,904, but a net surplus of £420,727.

1 April — A new Limited Stop OMO single-deck bus service (98) is introduced between Kingstanding Circle and New Street. The West Midlands Transport Study Group also appoint its Secretary as its full-time Chairman.

5 May — The Bromford Bridge Estate-Alum Rock service (26) is converted from OMO single-deckers to OMO double-deckers.

12 May — The Nechells service (43) is converted to one-man double-deck operation.

June — The 'B' prefixes on the Dudley Road group of services, operated jointly with the BMMO, are dropped. Rosebery Street garage closes. It opened as a tramcar depot in 1906 and received its first buses in May 1947.

2 June — The Ladywood service (95) is converted to OMO double-deckers. The sightseeing tours of the city also resume. This year there are four tours, of the southwest, eastern, southern and northern areas, but they are bedevilled by a labour dispute and wet weather. Despite running until 2 October, they carry only 5,106 passengers in total.

30 June — The Lozells via Wheeler Street service (69) is converted to one-man double-deck operation.

7 September — A second ad hoc Park-&-Ride service is provided in connection with the City of Birmingham Show at Handsworth Park. From car parks at Perry Barr Playing Fields and Hinstock Road, a total of 1,928 passengers are carried on 48 round journeys.

9 September — The Limited Stop OMO single-deck bus service (98), introduced on 1 April between Kingstanding Circle and New Street, is extended to Queslett Road, with an appreciable increase in passengers.

October — The Transport Act, 1968, becomes law. Under its terms PTEs are to be established in four major conurbations: Greater Manchester, Merseyside, Tyneside and the West Midlands, to co-ordinate and, where appropriate, subsidise public transport by road and rail. The PTEs will come into existence on 1 October 1969, and their operation and direction will be overseen by Passenger Transport Authorities (PTAs). Before 31 December 1972 each PTE must have prepared a plan 'to secure or promote the provision of a properly integrated and efficient system of public passenger transport to meet the needs of that area'.

1 October — With the success of OMO the Transport Committee has ordered 100 more double-deck buses for delivery in 1969. This order will cost £923,120 and application is made to the Finance Committee 'to borrow or otherwise provide' this money.

At 19 years, and still going strong, Leyland PS2/1 No 2257 was loaned to Potteries Motor Traction from 1 June 1969 to cover for temporary shortages. It is seen at Burslem depot on 22 June, in strange territory, but on a familiar service. Reloaned twice more, upon its return on 2 June 1970 the bus did not enter public service with the PTE, but became a tuition vehicle. *A. Moyes/IAL*

7 October — The City Circle service (19) is converted to OMO single-deckers.

9 October — As the Inner Ring Road develops there is less and less pavement space within the city centre, leaving fewer setting down places for buses. In response, from this date the terminus of the OMO Nechells service (43) is moved from Corporation Street to Bull Street, outside Lewis's. On 13 October the termini of the Witton service (39) and the Tile Cross, Great Barr and Queslett Road night services (14, 51 and 90) are also moved to Bull Street from Temple Row.

29 December — The Witton service (39) is converted to OMO double-deckers.

1969: BACK TO THE BEGINNING?

With just nine months to serve the city, Birmingham's Transport Department maintained its high standards to the end. A final delivery of buses, 67 Daimler CRG6LX Fleetlines (Nos 3814-80), with 72-seat Park Royal bodies, entered service. They were equipped for one-man operation from new. From 1 October 1969 the Department's assets came under the control of the newly formed West Midlands PTE, and the last General Manager, Mr W. G. Copestake, became the first Director of Operations.

January — The Town Clerk reports that final agreement has been reached with all the constituent authorities over the establishment of the West Midlands Transport Study Group.

24 February — A passenger is killed in an accident involving the central doors of an OMO double-deck bus on the Bristol Road.

4 March — The General Purposes Committee considers the distribution of appointments to the proposed West Midlands Passenger Transport Authority. Birmingham is to have nine out of the 24 Local Authority places on the

Although this story finishes with the formation of the PTE, for many in Birmingham something of the Corporation days was retained so long as rear-platform buses continued to be used on the Outer Circle service 11. This era ended on 28 October 1977 when ex-BCT Guy Arab IV No 2615, seen here, entered Acocks Green garage, and all similar buses were withdrawn. *IAL*

Authority. Accordingly nine representatives and nine deputies are nominated and appointed to serve on the Authority with effect from 1 April.

31 March — The last full annual accounts of the Transport Department show that in 1968/9 it had total working expenses of £9,965,402 and a total income of £10,591,764, all but £262,817 of which was produced by traffic revenue. A net revenue surplus of £171,175 was reported.

1 April — The West Midlands PTA begins to meet.

15 July — Reporting back on the fatal accident involving the central doors of an OMO double-deck bus on the Bristol Road, the Transport Committee notes that the door mechanisms on all such vehicles have now been modified so that the front pair cannot now be closed until the central pair have been closed.

13 August — The Minister of Transport makes the formal order transferring the various municipal transport undertakings in the West Midlands to the West Midlands PTE; it comes into effect on 2 September.

1 October — The control and assets of the Birmingham Corporation Transport Department come under the authority of the West Midlands PTE.

7 October — The Council's General Purposes Committee recommends the winding up of the Transport Committee and the transfer of its remaining functions, of testing vehicles and providing and maintaining bus shelters, to the Public Works Committee. This is agreed. The next item considered by the General Purposes Committee is a proposed study 'to examine the potential for developing rapid transit networks in the Birmingham area'. Isn't this where it all began 65 years ago?

Appendix. Birmingham Corporation Transport Vehicles in Service on 3 September 1939

1. TRAMS

At the head of each entry the following information is given: fleet numbers, class name, body maker, electrical equipment supplier, year entering service. Details of the seating capacity of the vehicles follows the convention (upper saloon/lower saloon).

1-20   **'Original bogie' cars UEC Co/ Dick Kerr & Co 1904**
Purchased to inaugurate the Corporation's tramway service in January 1904, these bogie double-deckers sat 56 (28/28). By 1939 they had been fitted with top covers (1904-5) and platform vestibules (1924-9).

21-70   **'Brill class' UEC Co/Dick Kerr & Co 1905**
Obtained in three batches, these four-wheel double-deckers sat 48 (26/22), and were all in service by June 1906. They were progressively fitted with top covers (from 1911 onwards) and with platform vestibules (1923-8). In 1924 cars 55-61, 63-4, and 68 were fitted with bow current collectors for use on the Lodge Road route 32. By 3 September 1939 only cars 43-4, 49-50, 53, 55, 59, 61, 63-4 and 67 remained in service.

71-220   **'Radial class' UEC Co/Dick Kerr & Co 1906**
Mounted on Mountain & Gibson radial trucks, these four-wheel double-deckers entered service from August 1906 to March 1907. They sat 52 (28/24) and were fitted with top covers from new and with platform vestibules progressively from 1923. By 3 September 1939 only cars 72-3, 75, 78, 80, 84, 86-7, 89, 92, 94-5, 98-99, 102, 105, 107-8, 117, 124-5, 129, 136, 139, 141, 147, 150-1, 154, 156, 159-60, 165-6, 169-70, 172, 176-179, 183, 185, 188-9, 191, 195-6, 198, 200, 203, 207, 209-11 and 220 remained in service

221-270   **'Brill class' UEC Co/Dick Kerr & Co 1906**
Sharing the same specification as cars 21-70, these entered service from March to May 1907. By 3 September 1939 only cars 221-2, 244, 248, 250, 259-63, and 266 remained in service.

271-300   **'Brill class' UEC Co/Dick Kerr & Co 1908**
With the same specification as cars 21-70 and 221-270, these entered service from March to April 1908, and had all been withdrawn by 3 September 1939.

301-360   **'301 class' UEC Co/Dick Kerr & Co 1911**
Four-wheel double-deckers, these cars entered service from April to June 1911. Seating 52 (28/24), they were fitted with both top covers and vestibules from new. Only cars 323, 335 and 346 had been withdrawn by 3 September 1939.

361-400   **'301 class' UEC Co/Dick Kerr & Co 1911**
Essentially an extension of the contract for 301-360, these cars had platforms which were 3in longer. They entered service from November 1911 to February 1912.

401-450   **'401 class' UEC Co/Dick Kerr & Co 1912**
Initially considered as an extension to the 301 class contract, these cars were very similar in specification, seating 54 (30/24). They entered service from August 1912 to March 1913.

451-2   **ex-CBT Co 1903**
Acquired in July 1911, these bogie double-deckers had been built at Kyotts Lake Road by the CBT Co in 1903. They were the longest cars operated in Birmingham, seating 71 (37/34), and gained top covers and platform vestibules in January 1926, remaining in service on 3 September 1939.

453-511   These numbers were allocated to ex-CBT Co cars, all of which had been withdrawn by 3 September 1939.

512-586   **'512 class' UEC Co/Dick Kerr & Co 1913**
Bogie double-deckers, these cars entered service from October 1913 to December 1914. With top covers and platform vestibules from new, they sat 62 (34/28), having their open balconies enclosed between 1926 and 1930.

587-636   **'587 class' Brush/BT-H 1920**
A modification of the prewar 512 class, with different body and equipment suppliers, these entered service from March 1920 to March 1921. They had their open balconies enclosed between 1929 and 1932.

637-661   **'637 class' MRC&W Co/ English Electric Co 1923**
Developed from, but similar too the 587 class, these 63-seat (35/28) totally enclosed cars entered service from October 1923 to January 1924.

662-681   **'662 class' Brush/English Electric Co 1924**
With similar bodies and identical electrical equipment, these 63-seat (35/28) totally enclosed cars entered service from March and April 1924.

682-701   **'662 class' Brush/English Electric Co 1924**
An extension of the 662 class order, these cars entered service from December 1924 to February 1925.

702-731   **'702 class' Brush/English Electric Co 1925**
Nearly identical to the 662 class, these cars sat 62 (35/27) and entered service from September 1925 to January 1926.

732-761   **'EMB Air-Brake cars' Brush/ English Electric Co 1926**
These 63-seat (35/28) totally enclosed cars were the first to be fitted with EMB Co air-brakes from new. They entered service from September 1926 to March 1927.

762-811   **'EMB Air-Brake cars' Brush/ English Electric Co 1928**
Developed from the above cars, this second generation had improved equipment. They sat 62 (35/27) and were distinguished by double the number of window panels on the upper deck to the lower one, and by being fitted with bow collectors rather than trolley poles. They entered service from September 1928 to February 1929.

812-841   **'M&T Air-Brake cars' Short Bros/English Electric Co 1928**
With bodies identical to the 762 class, these cars had Maley & Taunton bogies and air-brakes. They entered service from November 1928 to April 1929.

842   **Short Bros/English Electric Co 1929**
The first of two experimental lightweight aluminium-bodied trams, car 842 sat 63 (36/27) and entered service in November 1929.

843   **Brush/GEC Co 1930**
Birmingham's last new tram was another lightweight-bodied one which sat 60 (33/27) and entered service in September 1930.

2. TROLLEYBUSES

At the head of each entry the following information is given: fleet numbers, body maker, chassis maker, year entering service, registration numbers. Details of the seating capacity of the vehicles follows the convention (upper saloon/lower saloon).

1-11   **Short Bros./Leyland TB2 1932 OV 4001-11**
Taking the fleet numbers of most of the original trolleybuses, withdrawn in 1932, these Leyland four-wheelers seated 48 (27/21).

12-16   **Brush/AEC 663T 1932 OJ 1012-6**
Also taking the fleet numbers of withdrawn vehicles, these AEC six-wheelers seated 58 (33/25).

17-66   **Metro-Cammell/ Leyland TTBD2 1934 OC 1117-66**
These 50 six-wheeled Leyland vehicles seated 58 (33/25)

67-78   **Metro-Cammell/ Leyland TB5 1937 COX 67-78**
Four-wheeled Leyland vehicles which sat 53 (29/24).

79-90   **Metro-Cammell/ Leyland TB7 1940 FOK 79-90**
A further 12 Leyland vehicles which sat 54 (30/24).

3. BUSES

At the head of each entry the following information is given: fleet numbers, body maker, chassis maker, year entering service, registration numbers. Details of the seating capacity of the vehicles follows the convention (upper saloon/lower saloon).

1-337   Numbers allocated to vehicles withdrawn from service before 3 September 1939. In some cases these were reallocated to new vehicles, which are listed below.

338-367   **Brush/AEC Regent 1929 OF 3970-99**
Delivered on into early 1930, these Regents seated 50 (26/24), with the following remaining in service on 3 September: 340-3, 345-7, 349-50, 352-4, 356 and 358-67.

209, 338-9, 368   **AEC Regent 1930 OG 209, OG 3638-9, OF 8368**
Four vehicles, mostly out of sequence, being the first all-metal-bodied bus (209); two replacements for older vehicles (338-9) and an ex-demonstration model (368). All but 339, withdrawn in 1938, worked on past 3 September 1939.

369-443   **AEC Regent 1930 OG 369-443**
These Regents had bodies supplied by two makers: 369-408 being 48-seaters (27/21) by English Electric, and 409-443 to the same configuration by Vulcan. On 3 September 1939 the following remained in service: 369, 371, 373-81, 383-5, 387, 389, 391-404, 411-2, 418, 420-1, 423-5, 428-31, 433-6, 438, 440 and 443.

81-90   **Metro-Cammell/ Morris Dictator 1931 OV 4081-90**
These 10 Morris Dictator single-deckers seated 34.

444-503   **AEC Regent 1931 OV 4444-503**
A batch of Regent double-deckers, which seated 48 (27/21). Nos 444-483 had bodies by Short Bros, the remainder being by Metro-Cammell. Only 455 had been withdrawn by 3 September 1939.

47-50   **Metro-Cammell/**
Morris Dictator 1933 OJ 9347-50
These four Morris Dictator single-deckers had 34-seater bodies, and were renumbered 77-80 in 1935.

504-5   **Morris Imperial 1933 OC 504-5**
Two double-deckers with different bodies: 504 had a 51-seat (29/22) one by Brush, and 505, a 47-seat one by English Electric.

507-553   **Metro-Cammell/**
Morris Imperial 1933 OC 507-553
A batch of Morris Imperial double-deckers with 50-seater (28/22) bodies. Nos 519-20, 532, 536 and 553 were withdrawn in 1939.

554-563   **Birmingham Railway & Carriage Works/Daimler CP6 1933 OC 554-563**
Ten Daimler CP6 double-deckers with 51-seater (29/22) bodies.

208   **Metro-Cammell/**
Guy Arab 6LW 1934 OC 8208
A rebuilt demonstration model double-decker, by 1935 it had been fitted with a 54-seat (30/24) body.

564-578   **Birmingham Railway & Carriage Works/Daimler COG5 1934 AOB 564-578**
The first of many orders for Daimler COG5 double-deckers, these with 48-seater (26/22) bodies.

579-633   **Metro-Cammell/Daimler COG5 1934 AOB 579-633**
A similar batch to the above, with Metro-Cammell bodies.

634-693   **Daimler COG5 1935 AOG 634-693**
A further batch of 60 COG5 double-deckers, with 48-seat (26/22) bodies supplied by three makers: 634-673 by the Birmingham Railway & Carriage Works; 674-688 by Northern Counties, and 689-693 by Short Bros.

694-793   **Daimler COG5 1935 AOP 694-793**
One hundred COG5 double-deckers, with a split body order: 694-743 had 48-seater (26/22) bodies by Metro-Cammell; 744-784 similar ones by the Birmingham Railway & Carriage Works, whilst 785-793 had 54-seater (30/24) bodies by the same maker.

93   **Park Royal/AEC Q 1935 AHX 63**
A former demonstrator, this double-decker was acquired in November 1935 and reseated to a 56-seater (29/27) in 1936.

32-41   **Metro-Cammell/**
Daimler COG5/40 1936 BOL 32-41
Ten single-deck versions of the COG5 which were used as ambulances during the war.

94   **Metro-Cammell/**
Daimler COG5 1936 BOP 94
A 52-seater (28/24) double-decked demonstrator purchased in December 1936.

794-893   **Daimler COG5 1936 BOP 794-893**
Another 100 COG5s, with 794-843 having 54-seat (30/24) bodies by the Birmingham Railway & Carriage Works, and 844-893 having similar ones by Metro-Cammell.

894-963   **Metro-Cammell/**
Daimler COG5 1937 COH 894-963
A batch of 70 COG5s with 54-seat (30/24) bodies.

964-968   **Leyland TD4c 1937 COX 964-8**
Five all-Leyland double-deckers with 52-seater (28/24) bodies.

969-999   **Metro-Cammell/**
Daimler COG5 1937 COX 969-999
An extra 35 COG5s with 54-seat (30/24) bodies.

1000-1033   **Metro-Cammell/**
Daimler COG5 1937 CVP 100-133
A further 34 COG5s with 54-seat (30/24) bodies.

1034-1038   **Metro-Cammell/AEC Regent 1937 CVP 134-8**
Five more Regents with 54-seat (30/24) bodies.

1039-1138   **Metro-Cammell/**
Daimler GOG5 1937 CVP 139-238
A batch of 105 COG5s with 54-seat (30/24) bodies.

1139   **Metro-Cammell/**
Daimler COG5 1937 DON 439
A demonstrator on hire from March 1937, this had a 54-seat (30/24) body.

102-200   **Metro-Cammell/**
Daimler COG5 1938 EOG 102-200
Another 99 COG5s, with 102-50 having 54-seat (30/24) bodies by Metro-Cammell, and 151-200 similar bodies by the Birmingham Railway & Carriage Works.

211-295   **Metro-Cammell/**
Leyland TD6c 1939 EOG 211-295
A large order for 85 Leylands, with 52-seater (28/24) bodies.

1140-1235   **Metro-Cammell/**
Daimler COG5 1939 FOF 140-235
A further 95 COG5s with 54-seat (30/24) bodies.

1236-1269   **Daimler COG5 1939 FOF 236-269**
A final 34 COG5s fitted with 54-seat (30/24) bodies by: Metro-Cammell (1236); English Electric (1237); Park Royal (1238); Brush (1239); with the remainder by the Birmingham Railway & Carriage Works.

Information on vehicles entering service with Birmingham Corporation Transport after 3 September 1939 can be found within the main text.

The Prestige Se

Yorkshire Tra

John Banks

Photography by G H F Atkins

© 2000 J M Banks & G H F Atkins
ISBN 1 898432 21 X

Cover: An idyllic, traffic-free scene at Redhill, north of Nottingham, in September 1965. Yorkshire Traction No. **1230** (**XHE230**) was working the Yorkshire to London express service via Nottingham and Northampton. Number 1230 was a 1962 Willowbrook-bodied dual-purpose 47-seater on a Leyland PSU3/3R chassis.

Title page: A scene redolent of the 1930s and all that was best in prewar coaching. Yorkshire Traction's Leyland Tiger No. **431** (**HE6344**) moves purposefully over the stone setts of Nottingham's Huntingdon Street as it leaves that city on the express service to the North Riding seaside resort of Scarborough. The vehicle was a TS6 model with coachwork by Eastern Counties of Lowestoft and the picture was taken in October 1935.

Opposite page: The "face" of Yorkshire Traction in the mid-1950s, but the Leyland double-decker is not as uncomplicated as might be thought at first sight. It started life as a 1947 Tiger PS1 single-decker No. 733, registered AHE464, which carried a Weymann 32-seat front-entrance bus body. Double-decker No. **1046** (**JHE823**) was created in 1956 from the chassis of 733 and a new Roe 59-seat body, running thus until withdrawal in 1966.

Rear cover: In National Bus Company days the Company's No. **864** (**TDT864S**), a 1978 Eastern Coach Works-bodied Bristol VRT, was painted in a version of the 1930s livery with in-house advertising for excursions and tours. It was photographed in Barnsley in May 1980.

Below: Yorkshire Traction in force at the seaside. Scarborough's Westwood coach park in July 1963 had this impressive line-up of Willowbrook-, Alexander- and Metro-Cammell-bodied Leyland single-deckers, in for the day on a children's outing private hire.

INTRODUCTION

To a small boy with the - admittedly unusual - proper equipment of a family understanding of one of its member's minority interests (and in the writer's youth a keenness for buses *was* a minority interest), things might have been different. It was difficult for him *not* to be able to pursue that interest in his home town of Kingston-upon-Hull, where the fleets of Hull Corporation and East Yorkshire Motor Services were part of the daily round. Readers of earlier volumes in this series will have read of youthful voyages of discovery whereby the fleets of United Automobile Services, East Midland and Lincolnshire Road Car were discovered - wide-eyed - by the same small boy.

It was difficult, however, sometimes impossible, to break through the carapace of impatient family apathy when bus stations and depots in far-flung foreign lands such as Leeds, Doncaster or Sheffield were sighted. Such towns were not being visited, merely passed through on the way to somewhere else, and time spent at a standstill whilst buses were examined, tickets collected and crews pestered with questions to which they usually had no answer ("*I dunno, lad, I only drive 'em*"), was seldom granted.

Every now and again, though, often as the result of a bit of childish blackmail, things improved. There was a quarry on one of our routes to see relations. It was full of time-expired buses. Memory of their shapes suggests that they dated from the thirties, perhaps even the twenties, and I had longed to explore. It was too far to go on my bike so an alternative was sought. One year, for the school hobbies and handicrafts exhibition, several of us offered to produce a scrapbook of bus tickets. There was a hint, more then a hint, of that familiar parental-type incomprehension in the teacher's eyes as he reluctantly accepted our offer, but we were in business. The next time we passed that quarry I pleaded the scrapbook project. "Might there not," I wheedled, "be some tickets still in the ticket-boxes of the old buses?" Well, it was thin, very thin, but just about good enough to bring father's prewar Ford 8 to a creaking halt. "Ten minutes!" was the stern injunction. I returned three-quarters of an hour later, covered in dust and grime, with muddy shoes, happily clutching a fistful of prewar bus tickets, deaf to the inevitable recriminations. ("Where the Dickens d'you think *you've* been? Is this your idea of ten minutes?")

Doncaster and Sheffield were often on our line of route to visit relations in Nottinghamshire. I never was able to halt the expedition outside the fascinating bus garages, tram depots or bus stations which we would pass. Other towns, too, remained unexplored; memories had to be confined to what could be seen from a car passing by. Barnsley, in and around which the Yorkshire Traction Company Limited operated, came into this category. Although I often saw the Company's vehicles, I never in that era examined one close-up. One person who did, and from the dates of his photographs may occasionally have been in Barnsley on the same days I was passing through, a miserable captive, was the Nottingham photographer G H F Atkins.

Geoffrey Atkins started taking photographs in 1927 at the age of 15. Now in his late eighties, he still on occasion takes a camera with him on walks in his home town and has thus taken photographs in each of nine consecutive decades. Initially more interested in railways, Geoffrey would often in those early days photograph buses as a peripheral interest in the towns being visited for railway photography.

Visits to Barnsley began in the early thirties when a magnificent series of portraits of Leyland Cubs, Lions and Tigers, Daimlers and Dennises was begun. The series was continued through the thirties and after the war Yorkshire Traction's splendid fleet of Leylands was enthusiastically recorded. The earliest view in this book was taken in 1932 and the latest in 1988.

In those 56 years it was Geoffrey Atkins's intention to make a visual record of the coachwork fitted to Yorkshire Traction buses and coaches. The art of the coachbuilder is Geoffrey's main interest, although his collection includes traffic and general scenes as well as a superlative series of night shots (not, unfortunately, including YTC vehicles). His interest has always been towards the standard vehicles in company fleets. That is not to say that municipalites and independents are absent from his collection, but they take second place to company operators, particularly of the old BET and BTC groupings. The absence of independents may be partly explained by Geoffrey Atkins never having owned a car or motorcycle. All his photographic expeditions were done by public transport and a day out to, for example, Barnsley would naturally find him decanted from a train into in a bustling town centre, where company buses predominated.

4

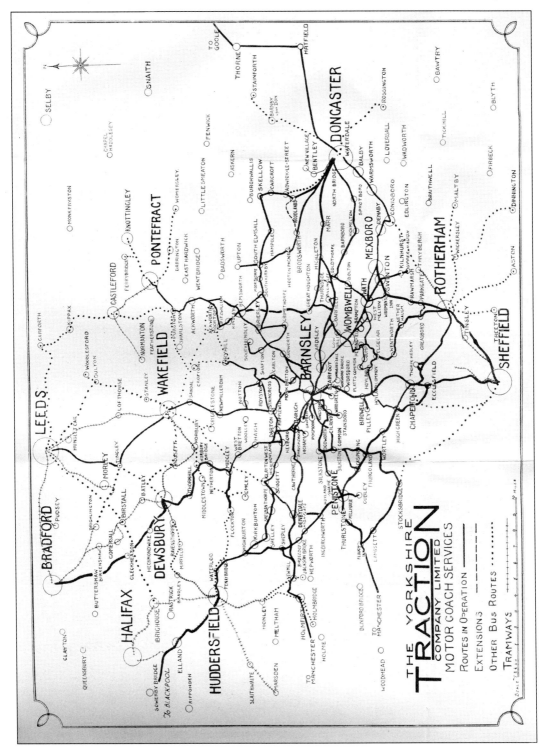

Having in 68 years achieved the consistency and colour of old parchment, this route map from Yorkshire Traction's 1932/3 Souvenir Guide survives to show us the Company's then operating area, centred on Barnsley, from Leeds in the north to Sheffield in the south and from Huddersfield to Doncaster on the east-west axis. Involvement in the provision of limited stop and express services broadened the Company's area of influence to such places as Manchester, Blackpool and London.

Enthusiasm for buses and coaches takes many forms and many millions of photographs have been taken, especially since the nineteen-fifties when lower-cost 35 millimetre cameras and film became readily available. Some enormous collections have been built up, in some cases quantity evidently having been preferred to quality. Geoffrey Atkins has never been the sort of photographer who tries to photograph everything in sight in an attempt to cover every vehicle in a favoured fleet. Sometimes he has been satisfied with one exposure of a particular type, for it has given him what he wanted - a satisfactory image of the coachwork. In many cases he has been tempted to a second and subsequent shot of the same type, perhaps to improve on earlier attempts or sometimes out of an affection for a particular design.

In days gone by the ASA rating of film was very low. Speeds as low as 25 or even 10ASA were common. Use of such film ensured the sharpness and clarity of much of Geoffrey's work. It also explains the frequent use of a low angle when the camera was placed on a low wall or other convenient surface for a time exposure when the shutter speed demanded by the lighting conditions was too slow for a hand-held exposure.

Geoffrey Atkins's pictures were never taken with publication in mind. It was the London material (to feature in the next *Prestige Series* album) in his collection that sparked off thoughts of publication and from that germ the idea of a series of albums grew. This has involved a number of visits to Geoffrey's home in Nottingham to tackle the job of what to include and what to leave out. Visits that are much enjoyed and warmly remembered. My ring on the doorbell just about dead heats with the kettle going on and, pot of tea and biscuits to hand, the work of choosing the pictures begins. It is always a joint effort, with Geoffrey making the case for some of his favourites over the years, and the writer pressing for others which appeal. There is seldom disagreement though there is always a mutual regret at what must be left out. As has been the case with the earlier volumes in this series, the prewar material forms the core of the Yorkshire Traction coverage.

My thanks then, as always, to Mr Geoffrey Atkins for making his collection and his unrivalled knowledge of coachwork available. Appreciation is again recorded for the expert help received from fellow enthusiasts Philip Battersby, John D Watson and Ron Maybray. They doubtless dread the postman's arrival or the telephone ringing at around the time a new *Prestige Series* album is in preparation, but they may take comfort in knowing that without their guidance, general and specific, the books would be the poorer. This time I also acknowledge with gratitude the help of Roy Marshall and Ken Braithwaite, who have read the proofs and offered sound suggestions for the improvement of the text. Ken has also provided the items from timetables and publicity leaflets. The publications of The PSV Circle and The Omnibus Society have proved invaluable in the preparation of these notes and the captions in the body of the book, and are gratefully acknowledged.

THE COMPANY

The southern part of the West Riding of Yorkshire, centred on Barnsley, is an area of rolling countryside, delightful parkland, wooded glades and tinkling streams. Over to the west it rises to majestic Pennine moorlands which seem almost to sweep the sky. Among its jewels are Bretton Park and Wentworth, Cawthorne Park and Ackworth, Brodsworth Hall, Nostell Priory and Holmfirth.

However, when you think of Barnsley, you must surely think of coal. Countless acres in this same area have been scarred by collieries great and small, their gaunt buildings, shale tips, railways and roads, and the blackness which seems to pervade everything. Centuries of mining have produced a hard-headed uncompromising people with unshakeable loyalties and hearts of gold. The harshness of life underground has been mirrored in the harsh appearance of their towns and villages, and sometimes even in their names. Who would feel a romantic magnetism in the names of Wath-upon-Dearne, Grimethorpe or Wombwell?

For the reader of this book, Wombwell is a reminder of another face of Barnsley, that of the bus dealer and breaker. Here the image is of a black yard on the site of a reclaimed tip or disused mine, full of buses, bits of buses, and alsatian dogs. Sometimes it is accompanied by the most primitive sort of aluminium smelting, using a gas canister and burner in a rickety old shed, and pouring the shining metal into sand moulds on the floor. Most bus enthusiasts know the names not only of Wombwell, but also of Carlton, Lundwood, Royston, Cudworth and the incomparably named Blacker Hill. Many have also been to them, sometimes just to look, and at other times to scour the yards for components in connection with a preservation project.

In this area of dramatic contrasts, the Yorkshire Traction Company and its predecessors have provided tram and bus services for almost a century and will celebrate a well-earned centenary in 2002.

In 1900 the Barnsley & District Light Railways Order was approved by Parliament. The British Electric Traction Company Limited formed a subsidiary to take advantage of the powers granted by the Order and thus the Barnsley & District Electric Traction Company Limited was registered at Companies House on 3rd March 1902. Trams ran on the Worsbrough and Smithies routes from November 1902 to August 1930. Many plans for other tram routes, for which the Company had the necessary powers, were stillborn. The growth of the fledgling motor bus quickened and strengthened to such effect that further investment in trams was deemed inadvisable. From a tentative start with the purchase of five motor buses in 1912, the use of non-electric vehicles increased so rapidly that by 1925 the fleet totalled 118 and the word "Electric" was eventually excised from the Company's name.

The title "Yorkshire Traction Company Limited" did not appear until 1929 when the Company was reorganised administratively during a rationalisation of the activities of the British Automobile Traction Company Limited (the BET's provincial public transport operating arm) and Thomas Tilling Limited, a major shareholder. As a consequence of this and also because the Barnsley company had broadened its operating area considerably by the late 1920s, the name Yorkshire Traction was introduced.

In 1929, as we have seen from the stories of other company operators dealt with in this series of books, the railway influence emerged. The London Midland & Scottish and the London & North Eastern Railways jointly bought in to Yorkshire Traction and became equal shareholders with Tilling & British Automobile Traction Company Limited. When in 1942 the BET and Tilling operations once more became separate, Yorkshire Traction became a BET company. The railway-owned shares were nationalised in 1948 and passed to the new British Transport Commission and thence to the Transport Holding Company in 1963. BET sold out to the THC in 1968 and on 1st January 1969 the gargantuan National Bus Company, formed

YORKSHIRE TRACTION
COMPANY LIMITED
ASSOCIATED WITH LNE & LMS RAILWAYS

TIME TABLE OF

MOTOR COACH

SERVICES

JANUARY to APRIL, 1936.

PRICE ONE PENNY.

of the former BET and Tilling companies, lurched into being with Yorkshire Traction as part of its portfolio of assets.

Across more than a half-century, from 1925 to 1978, Yorkshire Traction pursued a vigorous campaign of buying out competing operators as well as taking a one-third share, in 1927, jointly with the Yorkshire Woollen and West Riding companies, of County Motors of Lepton. When all three companies passed into the ownership of the National Bus Company the County fleet and operations were absorbed by Yorkshire Traction. The creation of the NBC and the common ownership thus established also caused Traction to absorb the Mexborough and Swinton Traction Company Limited.

Yorkshire Traction had a hugely varied network of urban, inter-urban and rural routes, works and colliery special services as well as extensive private hire and express operations. Its headquarters near Worsbrough had been purchased in the period when the original tramway was being constructed and included a depot for a dozen tramcars. Subsequent expansion into adjoining land provided space for a central depot and workshops and office space for administrative staff.

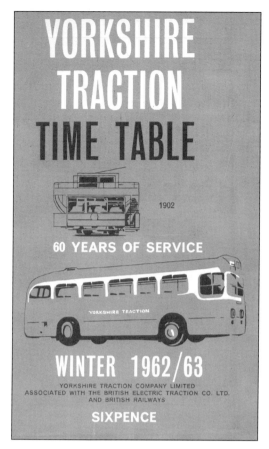

Diesel-engines were adopted in 1935 when the first of the type, fitted to Leyland Tiger TS7 chassis, were bought. Although some petrol-engined vehicles came later with the fleets of acquired operators, only diesels were bought new after 1935. At the outbreak of war in 1939 the Traction fleet was 286 strong, including 20 double-deckers. The low proportion of double-deckers was partly brought about by the unusually high number of low bridges in the Company's operating area.

Express services were operated to Blackpool and these became, with those of other operators, part of the Yorkshire to Blackpool Pool. The Birmingham and London services of a number of operators including Yorkshire Traction were also combined. The resulting celebrated Yorkshire Pool services from various starting points in Yorkshire were routed through Barnsley, which became the main interchange for the Pool.

In what is often thought of as the bus industry's golden age - the 1950s - the central depot housed 220 vehicles. The Company's bus station in Barnsley boasted then no fewer than 29 passenger boarding bays and the timetabled departures plus duplicates and workmen's services amounted to over 2,000 each day.

In that same era the position regarding independent competitors to some extent stabilised. Although most of them later succumbed to Yorkshire Traction, in the second half of the 1950s there were ten operators with timings on services where the Company was the major operator. Making, perhaps, a virtue out of necessity, friendly working relations were established and maintained with these operators. Coordination of timetables and interchangeable return ticketing were two examples.

When the BET sold its bus interests to the THC in 1968 Yorkshire Traction became wholly state-owned and part of the National Bus Company, under whose auspices it initially carried on much as before. There was participation in National Express and National Holidays activity and, in 1974 following the creation of the Metropolitan Counties of South and West Yorkshire, the Company's stage carriage network, which fell into and across the new boundaries, was coordinated with those of the respective Passenger Transport Executives.

When the NBC was privatised in 1985 a successful buy-out by management brought Yorkshire Traction back into private ownership. In 1988 the Lincolnshire Road Car Company was purchased from the remnants of the NBC, and the Newark operator W Gash & Sons was acquired shortly afterwards. Lincoln City Transport, privatised in 1991 through a combination of an employee buy-out and a major shareholding by Derby City Transport, was purchased in 1993.

The Scottish Bus Group was also disbanded as was the NBC, and Yorkshire Traction added Strathtay Scottish (founded in 1985) to its empire in 1991. There has been much activity in the Sheffield area since privatisation and in 1999 a foothold in the Capital via a stake in London Traveller was acquired.

These later activities are generally outside the coverage of earlier years from the camera of Geoffrey Atkins that graces the pages that follow. It should be noted that the book makes no claim to be either a fleet list or a comprehensive history of the Company.

John Banks
Romiley, Cheshire
May 2000

Above: The start of a Geoffrey Atkins visit to Barnsley. The train has departed, leaving him on Court House Station to assess what the day will offer. The weather on this 1951 summer day was glorious and it was clearly difficult to resist this remarkable view of the Yorkshire Traction bus station in which at least 17 buses are visible. The bus station was sandwiched between the now-closed Court House and Exchange railway stations.

Below: Almost two decades earlier, in April 1933, a similar arrival at Doncaster LNER station produced sunshine and a Yorkshire Traction vehicle in the shape of No. **225** (**HE4225**). This Leyland Lion PLSC3 of 1929 was amongst the first vehicles purchased by the renamed Yorkshire Traction Company Limited. Its centre-entrance 30-seat body was by Brush. Note the absence of a front registration number plate.

Above: A dull and rather smoky day at Doncaster station in April 1934 found No. **310** (**HE4752**) waiting to leave on the 90-minute service 21 run to High Green via Barnburgh, Mexborough and Hoyland. The bus was a Leyland Lion LT1, new in April 1930. It was fitted with 30-seat bodywork by Brush, of Loughborough.

Below: The United Automobile Services and East Yorkshire Motor Services volumes in this series revealed that Geoffrey Atkins photographed those fleets extensively in the resort of Scarborough during summer holidays there. There were also frequent visits to the parking area for private hire coaches on Marine Drive when visitors to the resort were put on film. YTC's Brush-bodied 1930 Leyland LT1 No. **313** (**HE4755**) was there in June 1932. Despite the season, the radiator had been well protected. Of note is the destination blind rather than a "Bible" indicator. The vehicle is in one of the experimental liveries of that period.

Above: 1931's Leyland Lions were the LT2 model. Leyland bodywork seating 30 was specified. Number **345** (**HE5229**) from the batch featured in another Doncaster railway station view in April 1933. It was working service 13 back to Yorkshire Traction's HQ town of Barnsley. This 75-minute journey ran via High Melton, Thurnscoe and Darfield.

>>> *Page 12:* The Yorkshire Services Pool in its glorious prewar incarnation. As part of the express run from Bradford to London in August 1933, No. **363** (**HE5640**) had called in at Huntingdon Street, Nottingham. The vehicle was a Leyland Tiger TS4 with 32-seat coachwork by Weymann which had been new to the Company in June 1932. The manner in which the route was advertised to the public by means of roof boards is in stark contrast to the absence of such vehicle-mounted information today.

>>> *Page 13:* In the early 1930s the Leyland stranglehold on Yorkshire Traction's vehicle orders was temporarily broken by first Daimler and then Dennis, though neither marque succeeded in doing more than slightly denting the Lancashire factory's predominance. The Daimler CP6 chassis was specified for a batch of six 28-seat coaches with Brush bodies in 1933. A year or so after delivery No. **371** (**HE5994**) was at Huntingdon Street, Nottingham acting as a duplicate on the London express service. Note the conductor's smock.

>>> *Page 14:* The magnificent series of portraits of Yorkshire Services Pool vehicles from the YTC fleet in the mid-1930s at Nottingham continues with an August 1935 view of one of the 1933 Dennis Lancet I service buses with 32-seat Brush bodies. Number **375** (**HE5998**) had been delivered new in May 1933. The headboard "EXPRESS DUPLICATE COACH" suggests that it had worked in as a feeder and was going no further south.

>>> *Page 15:* Small buses of 14 or 20 seats had been purchased in some numbers with acquired operators' fleets by both the renamed Yorkshire Traction Company and its predecessor the Barnsley & District Traction Company. An order was placed in 1933 for some Roe-bodied 20-seat Leyland KP3 Cubs to augment the small bus fleet at a time when many of the second-hand vehicles were being withdrawn, in some cases without being used or even repainted, as unserviceable. On a splendid summer's day in August 1935 No. **382** (**HE6005**) had run into Skegness on an express service from Barnsley. It was photographed at Drummond Road, Skegness waiting to leave on the return journey.

15

<<< Opposite page and above: A day at the races at Doncaster in September 1935 saw Yorkshire Traction present with a number of vehicles on private hire. Dennis Lancet No. **415** (**HE6328**) was an MCCW-bodied 32-seater which had been new in July 1934, two months after No. **418** (**HE6331**) which was a Leyland Lion LT5A bodied by Roe, also as a 35-seater. Number 415 had the only MCCW unit bought at this time, no doubt to test a metal-framed body.

Below: Nineteen-thirty-four's new vehicles included six Leyland TS4 Tigers with 28-seat front-entrance coach bodies from the Lowestoft coachbuilder Eastern Counties - formerly United and soon to become Eastern Coach Works. Number **426** (**HE6339**) is seen at Huntingdon Street, Nottingham in May 1952 *en route* for Birmingham. This smart 18-year-old, originally petrol-engined, had been fitted with a diesel engine in 1945, together with modified beadings and sliding window vents, as well as losing its roofrack.

<<< *Opposite page and above:* The 1934 Eastern Counties-bodied Leyland TS6 Tigers in original condition are represented in a busy summer Scarborough scene and in an urban Nottingham landscape. Number **430** (**HE6343**) was at Valley Bridge bus station in June 1935. The luggage rack which was part of the original specification of the coachwork is seen being filled with suitcases by the crew. Number **427** (**HE6340**) was heading for Harrogate when photographed in Huntingdon Street, Nottingham in October 1935. Newly erected traction poles for Nottingham Corporation's trolleybuses are evident.

Below: The following year's Tigers were TS7s. Number **471** (**HE6741**) was on express duties at Southgate Street, Leicester in August 1935. The vehicle had been new the previous June. It was one of ten fitted with Weymann 32-seat bodies, believed to have been all-metal, which had unusually styled windscreens.

20

<<< *Opposite page:* Number **479** (**HE6749**), the last of the 1935 Weymann-bodied TS7s, is seen at Barnsley in June 1936, awaiting departure for Sheffield with its conductor in nonchalant pose against the offside-front mudguard. Until 1938, when Barnsley's new bus station was opened (boasting such progressive features as a cafeteria and toilets with hot and cold running water), bus stands were located in various town-centre streets.

This page: The 1935 TS7 32-seaters also came with bodywork by Leyland or Roe. The Leyland version is seen above on brand new No. **481** (**HE6751**) at Marine Drive, Scarborough in June 1935. Coaches were banished from Marine Drive in the early postwar period. The Roe version was perhaps the most attractive of the three with a neater cab-front and windscreen treatment than the Weymann and a less austere destination box arrangement than the Leyland. Number **501** (**HE6771**) demonstrates in August 1936 at Huntingdon Street, Nottingham. Foglamps with orange lenses are apparent on several vehicles in this period.

<<< Opposite page: A broadside view of the Roe version of the 1935 32-seater. Number **491 (HE6761)** was at Waterdale, Doncaster in September 1935.

Above: Some of the 1935 TS7s were rebodied as 34-seaters by Weymann in 1950. Number **493 (HE6763)** is seen so equipped in another Waterdale, Doncaster view. This one dates from September 1953. Number 492, an identically rebodied vehicle, has been restored by the Company.

Below: By 1936 the streamlining craze was at its height. Cars, locomotives, radio sets, buses - very little escaped and even less could be said to have been the better for it, although this 1936 Roe-bodied Leyland Tiger TS7 was less offensive than some. Under No. **535 (HE 7133)**'s curly paintwork with orange waistband there lurked a completely standard bus body. It was at Barnsley in June 1936 having been new the previous March. Service 27 was jointly operated with Rotherham Corporation whose blue and cream Bristol saloons contrasted notably with YTC's Leylands.

Above: Nineteen-thirty-six also produced a pair of fine Burlingham-bodied 31-seat coaches on Leyland Tiger TS7 chassis. Here the streamlining was an integral part of the design rather than an obvious "add-on" accessory. Number **549** (**HE7147**) had been new in May 1936 and was photographed at Huntingdon Street, Nottingham in the following August.

Below: Roe bodywork appeared again in 1937 when Yorkshire Traction ordered twenty service buses on Leyland Tiger TS7 chassis. A further four were bodied by Eastern Coach Works. Number **557** (**HE7753**) was less than six months old in this Huntingdon Street, Nottingham view taken in August 1937. It was, despite its service bus seating, apparently going to London. There were only 32 seats, however, and they were well-upholstered. The Clayton destination screen allowed more than one blind to be held, the required blind being fastened to the lower roller when needed.

Above: Five more Burlingham-bodied TS7 coaches arrived in 1937. They were re-engined and rebodied in the late 1940s. The original petrol engines were replaced by Leyland 8.6-litre diesel units and Charles Roberts & Company supplied new 34-seat front-entrance service bus bodies. The last of them, No. **580** (**HE7776**), is seen at Barnsley in May 1956. It was withdrawn the following year. The long-vanished Court House railway station overlooks the scene from the background.

Below: Burlingham was again asked to supply coach bodies in 1938. A further three were delivered, this time with 30 seats instead of 31. The last of the three was No. **624** (**HE8525**), seen here at Derby, on its way to Birmingham, in May 1951. The vehicle was withdrawn later in the same year and its chassis frames and running units formed the basis of a Beadle reconstruction which became fleet number 971 (EHE381).

Above: Nineteen-forty's deliveries, all bodied by Eastern Coach Works, included a batch of 30 single-deck service buses on Leyland Tiger TS8 chassis. Burlingham were not asked to supply coachwork that year but might have taken some satisfaction when, in 1952, No. **676 (HE9530)** was fitted with the Burlingham coach body formerly carried by No. 466 (FV2658), a 1932 Tiger TS4 which had been acquired second-hand from Pride of the Road, Blackpool in 1935. This was No. 676's second rebodying. It had carried a Roe unit from 1947 until the Burlingham body was fitted. It was photographed at Huntingdon Street, Nottingham in August 1952.

Below: Six Leyland Titan TD5s with ECW 54-seat bodies also appeared in 1940. Number **664 (HE9518)** was at Barnsley in May 1950. The 14 miles west to the now-famous village of Holmfirth, high on the Pennine moors, must have been a spectacular journey on this magnificent machine.

Yorkshire Traction, as did many another operator, had perforce to accept chassis and utility body combinations which would never have been bought but for the War. The ubiquitous Guy Arab appeared in the fleet in 1943 and had multiplied to a total of 20 by 1945. This one, No. **719 (HE9916)**, was bodied by Northern Counties for 1944 delivery. Other utility bodies were supplied by Massey, Roe, Park Royal and Weymann. This one was photographed at Barnsley garage in June 1954. It was photographed at Barnsley garage in June 1954. This one shows various modifications from when delivered: additional opening windows (all sliding), large headlamps and shortened wings.

Again like a lot of other operators up and down the country, Yorkshire Traction resorted to rebodying when it was found that the wartime Guy Arab chassis outlived the utility bodywork. Twelve of the 20 were so treated by Charles H Roe who supplied both lowbridge and highbridge bodies. Number **714** (**HE9867**) represents the highbridge version. The rebodying was done in 1952 and the bus withdrawn in 1962. Thus the new body lasted longer than had the original. The picture was taken at Barnsley in August 1952. In the background is a Yeates-bodied Dennis Lancet III of Camplejohn Brothers.

As soon as Leylands were once again available, Yorkshire Traction returned to its prewar purchasing policy. The first postwar Leylands were five PD1 Titans with Roe 56-seat bodywork. Number **726 (AHE163)** was at Barnsley in May 1956. The vehicle alongside, No. **936 (DHE574)**, was a lowbridge Leyland-bodied Titan PD2 dating from 1951. Note the step in front of the radiator for the conductor to stand on to change the blind. Number 726 has been preserved.

Above: Large numbers of new Leyland single-deckers were ordered for postwar delivery. Forty-five Leyland PS1 Tigers appeared in 1947, with service bus bodywork seating 32 built either by Weymann or Roe. Number **735** (**AHE466**), seen here at Waterdale, Doncaster in June 1949, was one of the Weymann examples. It had been new in 1947. Separate service number indicators were a postwar feature, on single-deckers at first.

Below and >>> opposite page: Whereas the Weymann version was to the British Electrical Federation design on behalf of YTC and several other associated BET companies, the Roe version was a standard product which differed in many details, as shown by No. **753** (**AHE775**) at Skegness Lawn Motor Park in July 1949 and an unidentified example, also parked out of service, photographed at Union Road, Nottingham in October 1949.

Above: In 1948 the double-deckers were Leyland PD2/1 Titans. Five were delivered in March and these were the only vehicles added to the fleet in that year. The bodywork, to 56-seat highbridge specification, was supplied by Leyland. Number **777** (**BHE138**) was at Furnival Road, Sheffield in September 1949, operating service 65 to Barnsley. This was jointly operated with the British Railways-owned Sheffield JOC. Bus shelters made from gas piping and corrugated iron were a contemporary feature.

Below: Leyland PS1s continued to augment the single-deck fleet in 1949. Forty-eight were delivered with either Northern Coachbuilders or Brush 32-seat bodies. Northern Coachbuilders were originally to supply 19 bodies but only one was built, the balance going to Brush. Number **795** (**BHE456**), with Brush body, was at Barnsley in August 1953.

Above: Nineteen-forty-nine's new double deckers were a batch of six PD2/1 Titans for which Charles H Roe supplied 56-seat highbridge bodywork to a restrained, elegant design. Number **828** (**BHE758**) was at Leeds Central bus station in May 1950 waiting to leave for Sheffield on service 67. Geoffrey Atkins recorded that this was a "very dull" day and that the photograph was taken at one fiftieth of a second at f4.5. To compensate for the dullness, the print was "Azol-boosted".

Below: In the same month No. **830** (**BHE760**) was at Barnsley bus station. The signwritten boards in the background gave departure details for day excursions and coastal services. A group of Yorkshire Traction platform staff stands between the boards, no doubt putting the world to rights between journeys. Number 830 is about to continue its 2hr 50min stage journey on service 66 from Sheffield to Bradford. Both this and the 67 Sheffield to Leeds (2hrs 15mins) were discontinued following the introduction of the "White Rose Express" M1 motorway-based network in 1969. The 66 was joint with Sheffield JOC and Yorkshire Woollen, the 67 with Sheffield JOC and West Riding. Why an *8* mph limit in Barnsley bus station, and not 5 or 10?

<<< *Opposite page:* Leyland supplied the bodies on 1950's PD2/1 Titans. Number **843** (**BHE773**) was delivered in May 1950 and later the same month was photographed at Dewsbury on the joint service 66. The 1943 Weymann-bodied utility Guy Arab behind was No. **482** (**HD7308**) of the Yorkshire Woollen District fleet.

Above: Number **842** (**BHE772**) of the 1950 batch was also brand new in this second May 1950 view, taken at Barnsley depot. Note the painted-out side indicator box.

Below: It was not uncommon for operators to alter details on their buses in later years. Yorkshire Traction modified the destination screen arrangement on this 1950 Titan, making three boxes where one had sufficed before. Number **841** (**BHE771**) was ten years old when photographed at Barnsley in April 1960.

Above: Yorkshire Traction turned to Dennis Brothers of Guildford for a total of 30 chassis in 1949 and 1950 when Leyland Motors was having difficulty meeting all its UK customers' potential requirements, as all manufacturers were allocated steel to allow all to compete for orders, especially for export. Delivered in August 1949, No. **872** (**CHE375**) was a Lancet, one of six unusually combined with Windover coachwork. The front-entrance body had 33 seats. The photograph was taken at Huntingdon Street, Nottingham in May 1950 and the vehicle's destination screens described its journey as the "Midland Route" to London.

Below: Number **854** (**CHE346**) was one of 24 Brush-bodied Dennis Lancet 32-seat service buses. It was parked between duties at Barnsley bus station in August 1952.

Above: The Roe body in its lowbridge version is exemplified by one of the 1950 Leyland Titan PD2/1s at Doncaster in April 1955. Number **884** (**CHE615**) was one of a batch of seven of these 53-seaters. It was working to Barnsley via South Elmsall on service 11.

Below: Twelve Leyland Tiger PS1s came in 1950 with Brush 32-seat service bus bodies similar to those on the same year's Dennis Lancets illustrated on the opposite page. In this scene, part of a general view of the Huntingdon Street parking area in Nottingham, No. **887** (**CHE721**) stands next to the previous year's Windover-bodied Dennis Lancet coach **872** (**CHE375**). The photograph was taken at 10.45 on a dull morning in June 1952. The distinctive, historic building behind the Tiger was unfortunately demolished in later years. It is understood to have been a police station.

Above: Number **895** (**CHE729**), a 1950 Brush-bodied Leyland Tiger PS1, in an August 1956 view taken at Barnsley bus station. The picture is as interesting for the rear view of a Northern Counties-utility Guy Arab as it is for the PS1.

Below: Among the last deliveries for 1950 were six Leyland PS2/3 Tigers with Windover 32-seat coachwork similar to the 33-seaters on 1949's Dennis Lancets. The forward of the two ornamental flares looked rather odd when the sliding door was open. This is an August 1951 view at Huntingdon Street, Nottingham and No. **900** (**CHE855**) was waiting to leave for Doncaster. This chassis was rebodied by Roe as a double-decker in 1961.

>>> Opposite page: The first underfloor-engined vehicles arrived in May 1951. Brush-bodied Leyland Royal Tiger PSU1/9 No. **911** (**DHE342**) was a typical example. It was at Barnsley in August 1951.

39

The Windover coachwork on earlier half-cab, forward-engined coaches must have been satisfactory, for Yorkshire Traction asked the coachbuilder to supply the bodies for its first underfloor-engined coaches for delivery in May and June 1951. Or perhaps this was another BEF order. The chassis specified was the Leyland Royal Tiger PSU1/15 and the 37-seat bodies had centre entrances.

On separate occasions Geoffrey Atkins recorded fore-and-aft views of No. **924** (**DHE562**), the second of a batch of six. The front view *(above)* was taken at Derby in June 1954 whilst the rear was another Huntingdon Street, Nottingham picture, dating from July 1955.

Above: In the new decade of the 1950s Leyland Motors Ltd consolidated its hold on Yorkshire Traction's vehicle orders and it would be almost two decades before new vehicles on anything other than Leyland chassis began to appear in quantity. For 1951's lowbridge Titan PD2/1s, Leyland bodywork was also specified. Number **940** (**DHE578**), delivered in May 1951, was at Barnsley a decade later in April 1961, bound for the incongruously named "Grimethorpe White City". A variation ran to "Grimethorpe Red City". The ingenious radiator blind, with fan-shaped adjustable opening, appeared to be a permanent fixture. The triple front indicator was now standard for double-deckers.

Below: Both highbridge and lowbridge versions of the Leyland-bodied Titan PD2/12 chassis came in 1952. In this Leeds Central Bus Station view of April 1952, No. **954** (**EHE52**) was operating on the 67 service from Leeds to Sheffield. An ex-London Transport Feltham tram is in the background.

Above: The underfloor-engined revolution gathered momentum in the early 1950s, too, and Yorkshire Traction embraced it enthusiastically via the heavy, somewhat over-engineered Leyland Royal Tiger chassis for both service buses and coaches. Number **964** (**EHE165**), new in August 1952 and seen here outside the Yorkshire Traction office at Waterdale, Doncaster in September 1953, had Roe 43-seat bodywork on a PSU1/13 chassis.

Below: Leyland's order books had been full and more than one operator had turned elsewhere for chassis, sometimes - for example Middlesbrough Corporation - permanently, sometimes, as with Yorkshire Traction's Dennises illustrated on earlier pages, temporarily. By the early 1950s the situation had eased; even so, the use of serviceable engines and running units from withdrawn vehicles in Beadle chassisless bodies was a popular money-saving initiative which produced "new" vehicles at cut price. YTC's No. **972** (**EHE382**) used the units from Tiger TS8 No. 629 of 1939. It was at Nottingham on a gloomy day in August 1953.

Above: Sheffield United Tours disposed of some Duple-bodied 33-seat coaches in 1952. They had been new in 1947 but had not been put into service until two years later. We saw in an earlier volume in this series that, despite being a "Leyland" fleet, East Yorkshire took advantage of this opportunity, as did fellow BET operator Yorkshire Traction, who bought six, numbering them 965 - 970. Number **969** (**HWJ987**) was at Huntingdon Street, Nottingham in April 1953.

Below: Even more exotic was No. **975** (**EHE922**), new in April 1953 and photographed at Nottingham in the following August. Windover 39-seat coachwork graced a Leyland Royal Tiger PSU1/15 chassis. The vehicle was on an express run to Birmingham. The rear entrance was a short-lived phase.

Above: Nineteen-fifty-three's double-deckers were, as might have been expected, on Leyland Titan PD2/12 chassis. There were lowbridge and highbridge versions. The former was by Northern Counties and was perhaps the most attractive half-cab lowbridge design of them all. Yorkshire Traction's No. **979** (**EHE926**) demonstrates at Barnsley in August 1953.

Below: The highbridge version came from Charles H Roe, and the same claim might be made for it. Possibly the mismatched lower edges of windscreen and lower deck windows was all that detracted from the otherwise perfect symmetry of the design. Number **989** (**EHE936**) was photographed at Barnsley in June 1954. The Company's practice of adding an "L" or an "H" to the fleet number to denote the vehicle's height is evident.

In May 1954 Geoffrey Atkins recorded this scene at Barnsley garage in which nine buses are visible. The underfloor-engined vehicles were the prime attraction and three quite distinct types are represented. From left to right are No. 916 (**DHE347**), a 1951 Brush-bodied Leyland Royal Tiger; No. **1010 (GHE10)**, one of the Saro-bodied Leyland Tiger Cubs delivered in 1954; and No. **999 (EHE946)**, a 1953 Royal Tiger with Willowbrook bodywork.

Yorkshire Traction embraced the "dual-purpose" concept in the mid-1950s. Perhaps its most unusual outward aspect in this fleet was the provision of more or less identical vehicles with either front or rear entrance. Willowbrook built the 39-seat bodies on 11 Leyland PSUC1/1 Tiger Cubs for delivery between July 1954 and April 1955. Three had rear entrances, exemplified by No. **1026** (**GHE26**), seen *(above)* at Huntingdon Street, Nottingham in May 1955 on express duties to Birmingham. Windover-bodied Royal Tiger No. **975** (**EHE922**) of 1953 was alongside. The front-entrance version (of which there were eight) of the Willowbrook-bodied Tiger Cub is represented by No. **1036** (**HHE187**), at the same place in the same month *(below)*. These vehicles also evidence the Company's first short flirtation with matching fleet and registration numbers, soon abandoned.

The rebodying of single-deckers as double-deckers, or vice-versa, was not all that common. Of those companies making the attempt, Yorkshire Traction produced perhaps the most attractive of all such conversions when some Leyland Tiger PS1s were rebuilt and rebodied as 59-seaters by Charles H Roe. In the splendid portrait above, taken on one of the few occasions when the sun shone on Geoffrey Atkins's Yorkshire Traction photography, No. **1046** (**JHE823**), which was rebuilt from 1947 Tiger PS1 No. 733, stands alongside No. **719** (**HE9916**), a 1944 Northern Counties-bodied utility Guy Arab. The photograph was taken at Barnsley in May 1956, as was the view below, with the sun still shining, of No. **1047** (**JHE824**), whose donor vehicle had been No. 738, also of 1947. Number 1047 was on a Barnsley local service.

Above: A very rare non-Leyland in the Yorkshire Traction fleet of this period, seen at Barnsley in April 1960. There were two of these Beadle chassisless machines. This one, No. **1073** (**LHE141**), was the second, delivered in October 1956. The body had 45 seats and the livery was more or less reversed. In the second half of the 1950s YTC painted several batches of service buses thus for use on express services at peak periods during their first year or so in service. They would revert to bus livery at first repaint.

Below: August 1957 produced this rather grim, dull day in Scarborough, doubtless disappointing the residents of Barnsley who had ventured to the resort aboard Yorkshire Traction's No. **1080** (**LHE508**). The 1957 Leyland Tiger Cub PSUC1/2T was a Burlingham-bodied 41-seater to the "Seagull" design, one of the classics. Sister vehicle **1076** (**LHE504**) was alongside.

Above: Further transformed Leyland PS1 Tigers appeared in 1957. Again Charles H Roe was responsible for the rebodying, supplying 59-seat highbridge bodywork on a variety of rebuilt PS1 chassis originally registered in the AHE- and BHE-series in the late 1940s. Number **1085** (**LHE513**), seen here at Barnsley in May 1957, two months after its re-entry into service, was constructed from the chassis of PS1 No. 748 (AHE479) of 1947.

Below: In June 1957 twelve Leyland PSUC1/1 Tiger Cubs with Willowbrook 44-seat service bus bodywork arrived. A year or so later, in August 1958, No. **1100** (**LHE528**) was displaying its reversed livery at Barnsley. Behind the Tiger Cub was one of the splendid 1950 Windover-bodied PS2/3 Tiger coaches waiting to depart on an excursion.

Above: The underfloor-engined chassis for single-deckers seemed to have no challenger in the late 1950s. There had been designs with engines at the side and at the rear in revenue-earning service in various parts of the world for two decades, but British operators had opted firmly for having the engine positioned horizontally under the floor. The Leyland Tiger Cub, a lighter design than its heavy predecessor, the Royal Tiger, was Yorkshire Traction's choice and 1958 brought a large batch of Park Royal-bodied 44-seaters. Number **1108** (**NHE115**), with the cream and red livery, was at Huntingdon Street, Nottingham in March 1959 when less than a year old.

Below: Thirteen months later, in April 1960, No. **1124** (**NHE131**) was in the standard livery at Barnsley bus station. The Park Royal body was smoother, more rounded than the Willowbrook.

Above: In the midst of all the underfloor-engined service bus orders, the coach fleet had to be augmented from time to time. Plaxton was the preferred coachbuilder for six 41-seat PSUC1/2 Tiger Cubs delivered in March 1959. Number **1145** (**OHE718**) displays well the clean, rather understated lines of the Scarborough product at Huntingdon Street, Nottingham in May 1962.

Below: Perhaps the biggest change in British PSV operating practice has been the introduction of the rear-engined double-decker, capable eventually of being operated without a conductor. The Leyland Atlantean appeared in many fleets in 1959, heralding the new age. Yorkshire Traction was no exception, taking 12 in the December. Weymann 73-seat low-height bodywork, with the peculiar "lowbridge" seating arrangement to the rear of the upper deck, was fitted. Number **1155** (**RHE805**) was at Barnsley in April 1960.

Above: For 1960's intake of underfloor-engined service buses Yorkshire Traction turned to the Metropolitan-Cammell Carriage and Wagon Company for 45-seat bodywork on ten PSUC1/1 Tiger Cubs. MCCW also got the 1961 order for 13 similar vehicles. From that batch, No. **1173 (SHE161)**, in the cream and red livery, was at Barnsley in April 1961. The bus had been delivered earlier that month.

Below: Number **1184 (SHE172)** of the same batch was in the standard livery when photographed at Huntingdon Street, Nottingham in August 1963. The destination "Yews Estate" applied to Barnsley local service 108, so clearly the "Private" displayed in the lower screen was appropriate on this occasion.

Above: The rebodying of single-deckers continued into the 1960s, using Leyland Tiger PS2 chassis many of which had previously carried coach bodywork. Number 897 had been a Windover-bodied 32-seater and in 1960 its chassis was transformed into No. 1187 (**THE187**), seen here, after renumbering to **783**, at Barnsley garage in April 1972. The fleet renumbering had taken place in 1967. The 63-seat forward-entrance bodywork on these vehicles was supplied by Northern Counties.

Below: A similar exercise in 1961 saw County Motors, Lepton No. 84 (EVH212) rebuilt into the new No. 1194 (**YHE194**), this time with rather ungainly, angular Roe bodywork. again seating 63. This bus was renumbered **790** in 1967 and was photographed in an experimental livery at Barnsley in June 1968.

Above: Maximum-length double-deckers in 1961 came in the shape of new Leyland PD3A/1 Titans, also bodied by Northern Counties with forward entrances, but now as 73-seaters with enclosed radiators. Number **1204** (**VHE204**), was at Barnsley in June 1963. Note the illuminated advertising panel with in-house publicity.

Below: Sporting a front-end design that would have been more at home on an American car of the period, which yet managed not to seem mismatched with the restraint of the rest of the design, the Burlingham coach body of the period found favour with a number of operators up and down the country. There were six of these 41-seat coaches, licensed in June 1961, of which No. **1211** (**VHE211**) is seen engaged in Yorkshire Services express work at Huntingdon Street, Nottingham in May 1963.

Above: Alexander bodywork was chosen for some 45-seat service buses for delivery in 1962. A batch of six, new in February of that year, is represented by No. **1216** (**WHE216**) seen at Barnsley in the following April with two double-deckers none too neatly parked behind it.

Below: The first of the batch, **WHE212**, originally No. 1212 but by then renumbered **502** in the 1967 renumbering scheme, was rebodied by Alexander in February 1968 with a Y-type design more usually associated with vehicles built to coach specification. It remained a 45-seat bus, however. The rebodying had followed the vehicle's destruction by fire in Barnsley bus station - almost on the spot occupied by No. 1216 *(above)* - the previous year. It was at Barnsley in June 1968 picking up passengers for service 20 to Manchester.

Above: Northern Counties bodywork was favoured for high-capacity double-deckers in 1962 and the chassis remained conventional rather than being further examples of the Atlanteans bought in 1959. Number **718** (**XHE225**), originally numbered 1225, was at Barnsley in May 1967 and demonstrates the enclosed radiator and forward entrance specification of the 73-seat bodywork.

Below: The following year saw yet more Leyland Tigers rebuilt and rebodied as double-deckers. Number **718** appears again alongside 1963's **798** (**YHE247**) which was a 63-seater and retained the exposed radiator of the vehicle from which it had been rebuilt, a Tiger PS2/5 which had been acquired from the Yorkshire Woollen District fleet. YHE247 had originally carried fleet number 1247. The picture is a May 1967 Barnsley view.

Above: In the 1960s Yorkshire Traction's share of operations on the Yorkshire Services moved decisively towards maximum length vehicles, epitomised by this 47-seat dual-purpose Leyland Leopard with Willowbrook coachwork, new in 1962. Fleet number 1232 when new, **XHE232** had been renumbered **202** by the time of this October 1967 photograph of it at Huntingdon Street, Nottingham on the Bradford service.

Below: Leyland Leopards with more comfortable coach seating came in 1962 for the London services. Plaxton received the order for the 49-seat bodies on three such vehicles which introduced reversed registrations to the Yorkshire Traction fleet. Number **1254** (**1254HE**), on a run from London to Huddersfield, features in a Nottingham scene of April 1963.

Above: Fifty-three seats were possible in basic service-bus versions of the 36ft-long vehicle. Marshall, of Cambridge, won the order for six such 53-seaters in 1964 on Leyland Leopard chassis. On a damp Barnsley day in June 1964 No. **1264** (**3264HE**) was waiting to take up a timing on service 42 to Ryhill Station, which had ceased to see regular passenger trains as long ago as 1930.

Below: The registration numbering system underwent another upheaval in the 1960s when the infamous year-letter system was foisted on to the country. Although it started in 1963 with "A", most authorities adopted it in 1964 with "B" and a few held out until 1965 and "C". The first appearance of it in the Yorkshire Traction fleet was on 1965's deliveries, including **CHE302C**, originally No. 1302, later **370**, a Willowbrook-bodied dual purpose 47-seater on a Leyland Leopard chassis. The vehicle was rebuilt, as seen here, as a 53-seat service bus in 1971. It was at Wombwell garage in April 1972, sporting a rather gimmicky, not easy to decipher "YT" logo, which was mercifully not put into general use, no doubt as the result of the onset of NBC corporate liveries.

Above: The Leyland Atlantean had a tentative start in the Yorkshire Traction fleet. The first batch had come in 1959, the second not until 1966. Leyland Motors were doubtless unworried in this case, for they were selling front-engined Titans to the Company instead. Northern Counties bodies were ordered for the 1966 machines, of which No. **1338 (FHE338D)** is seen at Barnsley bus station when brand new in June 1966.

Below: The dull weather that dogged Geoffrey Atkins's Yorkshire Traction photography followed him to the Capital for this view at Victoria Coach Station in May 1971. The photographer rose to the challenge in a picture with considerable impact of No. **15 (JHE615E)**, a Plaxton-bodied Leyland Leopard 49-seater which was the first vehicle to be numbered from new in the 1967 scheme. "E" registrations in 1967 were issued only from 1st January to 31st July, presaging the idiotic adoption of 1st August for the annual letter-change.

Above: Operators wedded to the Leyland marque had little choice other than to order Atlanteans as the 1960s drew to a close, for there was no other double-decker available following the phasing out of the Titan PD3. Significantly, Yorkshire Traction tried the Daimler Fleetline in 1968 as well as ordering further Atlanteans. Similar 75-seat bodies by Northern Counties were specified for both types. This is one of the Fleetlines, No. **643** (**NHE43F**), at Barnsley in May 1973.

Below: Four 75-seat Willowbrook-bodied Leyland Atlanteans added some variety to the fleet in 1969, for they were diverted from Devon General and ran in that operator's dark-red and cream livery for about two years. Number **750** (**RHE450G**) represents the quartet. It was at Barnsley in June 1971, by then in YTC livery.

Above: A June 1969 scene at Barnsley depot includes one of that year's Marshall-bodied Leyland PSU4 Leopards. Number **518** (**RHE518G**) had been in service for some three months. It was a 45-seater, seen here ready to go out on a schools service.

Below: On the same occasion No. **658** (**RHE658G**) was even newer, having entered service the previous month. 658 was a Leyland Atlantean with Northern Counties 75-seat bodywork which featured panoramic side windows on both decks. Service 40B to Gilroyd was a recent introduction to the timetable.

Above: Daimler Fleetline single-deckers were something of a novelty in 1970. The use as a single-decker of a chassis intended primarily for double-deck bodywork, when there were suitable single-deck chassis on the market, caused much interest. What was the more interesting was that Yorkshire Traction's first three single-deck Fleetlines were fitted out as dual-purpose machines. Marshall built the 45-seat bodies, as demonstrated by No. **230 (THE230H)** at Barnsley in May 1970. This batch of buses had been ordered by Mexborough & Swinton prior to that company's demise. Number 230 was working a relatively short-lived variant of the White Rose Express network: Mexborough to Leeds via Barnsley.

Below: A more conventional addition to the fleet in 1970 - though of a type perhaps not all that common in the big company fleets apart from Ribble - was No. **24 (THE924H)**, a Plaxton-bodied 49-seat coach, seen at Rawmarsh garage in April 1972.

Above: Other 1970 vehicles with what looked and felt like coach seating were classified as "dual-purpose". These were a trio of Alexander-bodied Leyland Leopards, of which No. **232** (**UHE232H**) is seen at Pond Street, Sheffield in June 1971, whilst working the X33 White Rose Express service from Sheffield to Bradford.

Below: Alexander also bodied nine Daimler Fleetlines as dual-door 45-seaters in 1970. One of these unusual vehicles, No. **365** (**WHE365J**), was photographed at Rawmarsh garage in April 1972.

Above: Number **21** (**NWW110E**) was a former unit of the Mexborough and Swinton Traction Company fleet, absorbed by Yorkshire Traction on 1st October 1969. It was a Leyland Leopard with what was among the handsomest of contemporary coach bodies, the "Commander" built by Duple Northern. The 49-seater had been new in March 1967 and was photographed at Rawmarsh garage in April 1972.

Below: In a photograph taken in July 1988 outside the Lincolnshire Road Car Company garage in Lincoln soon after the acquisition of LRCC by Yorkshire Traction, Bristol VRT/Eastern Coach Works 77-seater No. **819** (**SHE819M**) displays both companies' fleetnames. The vehicle had been new to the Yorkshire Traction fleet in June 1974. It was newly repainted in Yorkshire Traction's first post-NBC livery, although the fleetname style was a development from that adopted on privatisation.